I0485328

A rebellious teenagers guide to starting a landscaping & lawn care business.

Learn how to harness your energy and make money.

When you are a teenager you have a lot of rebellious energy. Why not take that energy, harness it to be productive, and make money! This book will show you how to succeed in starting your own landscaping & lawn care business.

By Steve Low

Host of The GopherHaul Lawn Care Business Show

and the Gopher Lawn Care Business Forum.

Table Of Contents

Believe in yourself: 15

Direct your energy towards personal growth: 21

Get started today with baby steps: 25

Be a rebellious attention getter: 43

Create the business you want: 49

Getting started: 55
How to choose the right business name: 58
How many lawn care accounts can a 1 man crew maintain: 68
5 simple ways to improve your lawn care business: 71
Business loans to get started: 74

Lawn care business insurance: 77

Creating a business plan: 82
Lawn care business startup cost: 90

Find a niche and you will find profits: 93
Is aeration a good niche: 103
How much money can a solo lawn care business owner make:
106

Equipment: 113
Equipment advice from a 15 year old business owner: 117

Don't buy too much lawn care equipment when you start: 121
A quick way to calculate equipment operating costs: 123
Choosing the right snow plow: 125
Open or enclosed landscape trailer: 127
Are leaf sweepers a good option: 130
How best to use a mower vac: 132
How long should a commercial lawn mower last: 135

How to price and estimates jobs: 139
Charge by square foot or man hour: 143
Should I charge for estimates: 144
The best way to bid an apartment or condo complex: 145
How to price retaining walls: 147
How to bid on cemeteries: 151
Getting started offering holiday decoration: 153
Getting started offering gutter cleaning services: 156
How to charge for snow plowing: 159
Should you raise or lower your lawn care prices in winter: 162
Make money winterizing irrigation systems: 165
Why the cheapest lawn care bid doesn't always win: 168
Don't try to compete with $15 bucks a cut: 171
What's more profitable, small or large yards: 174
How to price and trim hedges: 178
How to estimate and market stump grinding: 181
Create a check list to win over commercial jobs: 183
How to price a fall leaf cleanup: 185
Offer a home safety inspection: 188
What freebies work to get lawn care contracts signed: 192
The benefits of lawn care contracts: 194
The danger of large lawn care accounts: 197

Dealing with lawn care customers: 201
Questions to ask new customers who call you: 205
Thank you letters to customers: 207

Planning lawn care customer base goals: 211
New lawn care customer welcoming kit: 213
How to get 30% more lawn care customers: 214
Why customers are canceling service and resolving it: 217
How to collect on overdue accounts:

Dealing with employees: 225
How to make the jump from one crew to two: 228
What keeps your lawn care business small: 230
Incentives to get employees to sell more: 232
What to train your lawn care employees: 234
What every lawn care employee should be taught: 236
How many lawns are you cutting with a 3 man crew: 238
Hiring employees for your lawn care business: 240

Why lawn care businesses fail: 245
Damaging customer's lawns:
Wasting money on ineffective ad designs: 254
Not varying your direct mail campaign: 257
Not talking to your customers: 259
Not offering services all year long: 261
Not knowing the average direct mail response rate: 263
Not striping lawns when you can: 265

Special thanks to Gopher Lawn Care Software.

This book would not have been possible without the help and guidance from all our friends and business owners we have met over the years on our Gopher Lawn Care Business Forum as well as others.

Also thank you to the staff at Gopher Lawn Care Business Software for making all of this possible.

Lawn Care Software
PROBLEM: Scheduling & billing repetitive jobs is tedious and time consuming.
SOLUTION: Gopher Billing & Scheduling Software allows you to Quickly and Easily schedule jobs and create invoices.

Gopher Landscape Billing and Scheduling Software simplifies the task of scheduling your lawn care jobs and billing your customers. Simply set up your jobs at the beginning of the season and let Gopher handle the rest. With Gopher, you can print out a list of scheduled jobs for each day and then automatically print invoices after those jobs have been completed.

Download your free trial of Gopher Billing & Scheduling Software at http://www.gophersoftware.com

Continue your reading.

I have more great information on running a lawn care business in my other books, **"Stop Lowballing! A Lawn Care Business Owner's Guide To Success."**

Some of the topics discussed in the book: - How to start up your lawn care  business. - Finding your niche and finding profits. - Lawn Care Equipment. - Pricing & Estimating Lawn Care Jobs. - Dealing With Customers. - Dealing With Employees. - Lawn Care Marketing Secrets. - Lawn Care Business Tips. - Getting Commercial Accounts without commercial references. - Pitfalls of Commercial Accounts. And more.

The GopherHaul Lawn Care Marketing & Landscaping Business Show Episode Guide.

Topics discuss include: How to raise start up capital. Seasonal marketing ideas. What to do when your largest client leaves? What's better to use, postcards or brochures? How to build your customer base with referrals? Gain one customer then lose one customer. How to stop it? How to pre-qualify customers when they call? How to bid jobs. What should you include in a commercial lawn care bid? What newspaper ads work best? How to buy a lawn care business. Tips on buying used lawn care equipment. And much more.

How to get customers for your landscaping and lawn care business all year long. Volume 1.

Anyone can start a lawn care business, the tricky part is finding customers. Learn how in this book.

New lawn care business owners were polled and 33% of them said the toughest part about running their business was finding customers. This book shows you how to get new lawn care customers. Don't start from scratch and try to re-create the wheel. Learn what works and what doesn't.

Volume #1 discusses: Getting started, choosing a business name, harnessing employees to sell, community marketing ideas, free rentals to offer, hosting events to get exposure, volunteer projects to build goodwill, how to get residential and commercial customers (including sample letters). Bikini lawn care, getting in your local paper, marketing on price, publicity stunts & media attention, organic lawn care marketing, reaching out to realtors, turning hobbies into marketing ideas, seasonal marketing ideas that work.

How to get customers for your landscaping and lawn care business all year long. Volume 2.

Anyone can start a lawn care business but most get stuck finding customers and they give up their new venture too quickly. Why struggle trying to learn how to gain new lawn care customers the hard way? This book gives you lawn care marketing ideas that are being used by your competitors. It also talks about what marketing ideas don't work.

Volume #2 discusses: The most effective lawn care business marketing methods. How to track your ads, the best ways to utilize: billboards, brochures, business cards, buying lawn care customers, clubs & organizations, coupons & gift cards, co-marketing, door hangers, going door to door, flyers, internet marketing, lawn signs, customer letters, direct mailing, newsletters, newspaper ad, phone book advertising, phones & telemarketing, postcards, referrals, sports, testimonials, trade shows, truck & trailer advertising, word of mouth.

The Big Lawn Care Marketing Book

This book contains 470 pages of marketing ideas to help your lawn care & landscaping business grow.

The Big Lawn Care Marketing Book contains volume 1 & 2 of my other books "How to get customers for your landscaping and lawn care business all year long."

The landscaping and lawn care business plan startup guide.

If you ever had thought about starting your own lawn care or landscaping business but weren't sure how to go about putting together a business plan, this book will show you examples of lawn care business plans created on the Gopher Lawn Care Business Forum. The author of this lawn care business book is the host of The GopherHaul Lawn Care Business Show and the Gopher Lawn Care Business Forum.

Inside is a step by step guide on how to make a landscape or lawn care business plan with real life examples including income and expense projections as well as customer acquisition goals. This lawn care business book is a great tool to help you improve your odds of finding success.

How to use Gopher Lawn Care Business Billing & Scheduling Software.

Learn how to manage your lawn care and landscaping business easier with this powerful software.

You can order these books through the following websites:

http://www.gophersoftware.com

http://www.gopherforum.com

http://www.amazon.com

Believe in yourself

Belief. It's an interesting way to get started isn't it? Believe in yourself.

One of the things you just got to love about the rebel who starts their own business is that most of the time, they believe in themselves more so than any other group. Are they suicidal? Are they crazy? Do they just not care? Well, I like to think of them as people who would be unfulfilled in life unless they were able to be free and explore.

In a country that prides itself on being capitalistic, not much time is ever really spent on teaching these young rebel explorers how to hone their craft. Not much time at all. After talking with business owners I have met over the years, I can't remember many at all who had classes where a teacher taught them how to be rebels. Can a teacher really teach one how to be a business rebel? Well, it is possible if they happen to work within a curriculum with the goal of turning out independent thinkers. More often than not though it seems school systems are designed to press and pump out carbon copies, each and every school year.

Quite simply there is more of a demand for workers than there is for business rebels and therefore school systems are set up to fill these needs. School curriculums are mostly standardized. Creative thinking and rebellion is not high on the educational priority list.

Thankfully though, there have always been a small percentage of the kids out there who really enjoyed rebelling. Kids who tested the boundaries and tested the limits of what they could or couldn't do. Sadly many times these kids drop out of school or end up in jail. They push things too far. They lack direction and focus. It's such a shame.

Can you become a wildly successful business rebel without a high school or college degree? Yes you can. Many wildly successful business owner rebels have never finished school but looking back, I bet you many of them wished they did. Think of school as a challenge. Challenge yourself to meet their requirements. Stay in school and get the highest level of education you can. Think about this, wouldn't it be a great challenge if you could find your way through the system and then after you made it out, with your degree in hand, prove them all wrong, by becoming wildly successful? I think that would be a lot more fun.

It seems many business rebels, never felt those warm and fuzzy vibes from their authority figures. Many rebellious students look at their authority figures and see automatons. They see cogs in a wheel. They ask themselves, do I want to emulate these people? Nah not really. I'd rather have fun, explore, and enjoy my life. If this is you and you are going to be a rebel, you better get paid or you won't be able to rebel for long.

If you are sitting there wondering if you have what it takes to make it, to rebel and get paid doing it, I believe you do. I believe anyone can if they want to do it. But doing so sometimes just goes against all we have learned. All we have been trained to think. It can be really tough when you are concerned what others will think about you. What if you fail at your first attempt and they all laugh? Will you be able to pick up the pieces and move forward? My view is don't be concerned with what others think. You know why? As important as it seems right now at this very moment, it will mean nothing in a year or two or five or ten or twenty.

Always consider the source of who's judgment you are concerned with. Look at their life. Ask yourself, would you want their life? Would you trade places with them? Would you like to be who they are? If the answer is no, then don't let their judgment of you, misguide you.

If you allow yourself to believe in yourself, you will be able to take that with you, your entire life. Where ever you go.

One of the strangest things about business is that quite often, to be successful, one must do things that seem counter intuitive. These things go against what is perceived as the correct path. Then you must do these things for a period of time no one would ever consider doing it for.

Rebels defy common logic. They defy common sense. They defy authority figures. They take it to a place where very few care to ever tread. The have a wild streak in them and are a bit crazy. This might explain why so many small business owners are also interested in other potentially hazardous activities. These type of rebels run into burning buildings when everyone else is running out. They will jump out of perfectly good airplanes for the thrill of it. This behavior goes against the grain. It goes against the heard mentality. It is also exactly what you need to succeed as a rebel entrepreneur.

Business is really a playground for rebels. I hope this book will help those of you out there who are rebels and want to direct your energy into positive directions and harness it. To own a business that makes a profit and allows you a fun filled life is the ultimate for a rebel business owner. So that is why I say, if you're going to be a rebel, you better get paid or you won't be a rebel for long.

You can achieve your wildest dreams and then some. So believe in yourself. Dream and dream BIG.

Direct your energy towards personal growth.

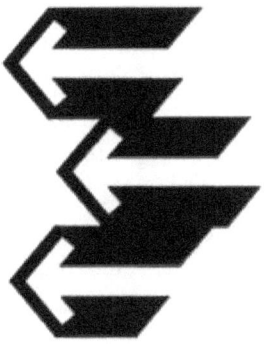

A short time ago I found myself having a conversation with a good friend of mine. Throughout the conversation he beat himself up and then went on to beat up the world.

He just got back from buying a used washer and dryer he found listed online. A homeowner who posted the items for sale had invited him over to check out the appliances and see if he wanted to buy them.

As he drove off to this house, he found it out in the woods. A beautiful house at least 5,000 square feet in size. It was much larger than his. This house was built on a few acres of property. Various pieces of construction equipment were parked on a large paver stone driveway. Along with the bobcat and backhoe were new cars as well. The homeowner owned a construction business and no longer needed his 1 year old washer and dryer because he was going to buy a new stainless steel set. For $1,200, my friend was able to walk away with this used washer and dryer. This was going to be a gift for himself and his wife.

After he got back home he sat down and had a chance to reflect on the evening's events. "How the hell did this guy get such a big house?" he asked with exasperation. "I mean how the hell did he do that? He wasn't a very bright guy at all." In fact my friend felt superior to him in many ways. And here he was handing over, $1,200 for used appliances. I mean what the heck!

"I work hard. I work hard everyday and I don't feel appreciated by my boss. I don't feel appreciated by my wife. I don't feel appreciated by my kids and here I am handing over my hard earned money to a guy who doesn't even need it. Where the hell did I go wrong and he go right?" he asked rhetorically.

After listening to him vent for a while I thought to myself isn't this a great country? I mean isn't it great? To see it like that you have to take a step back and say to yourself, you may never know how certain people made their money. Did they earn it? Did they inherit it? Did they win the lottery? You may never know. But what you do need to know is you need to be happy. You have to focus on YOU! Don't get mad at them. That's not going to help you or your situation. You have to get happy with you. And you know what? You can do this.

Sports heroes like basketball star Michael Jordan are gifted and talented. Nothing was handed to them except maybe good genetics. Such people have practiced their butts off and because of that, they get very good at what they do. In our capitalist society you can get money through many avenues. It's not necessarily based on you being talented. But finding what your talent is and leveraging it is a path to success many have taken.

What is your talent? If you find your talent and practice your butt off, there is a very good chance you will be happy with the results. At the very least you will find happiness in practicing what it is you enjoy. If you want to be happy, remember it's the journey you must enjoy and not just the destination.

My friend needs to take all that energy he has and focus it on his personal growth. It's easier to do this by taking baby steps in that direction. Small changes here and there will ultimately lead to a big change over time. Don't get mad at the outside world, it is a waste of your energy. Redirect that energy towards personal growth.

Get started today with baby steps.

Let me share with you some more experiences and stories of those who have walked before you.

I have found the best business ideas and the ones that will most likely be successful are the ones you can start today. The ones you can start right now. So go get a note pad and pen and create a list of services you can offer right now. Can you cut lawns? Can you trim a tree? Can you paint a house? Can you clean sewer lines? Can you baby sit? If you want to make a product, how about can you create arts and crafts? Make a list. Make it as long as you can so you have a better choice.

Making a list of services you can offer may be easier to get started with than making a list of products you can sell. Why? Because making a product is a more involved process that may take more resources than you have when you are starting up. Developing and making a product is much more cash intensive than performing a service. It is so much easier to sell a service and get a business up and running selling a service than selling a product because you will get immediate cash flow with a service.

What does that mean? It means if you cut a lawn today for $20, you will get paid $20 today. Now if you try and sell a product, you have to make that product and it's going to cost you money. Then it's going to sit there until you sell it. Then once you sell it, you have to support the product. You have to deal with the product breaking. You have to deal with refunds and tons of other issues. It's easier to get a service business started any day.

Once you make your list, ask yourself which ones would you enjoy performing the most? Which would be the easiest for you to start? I would advise against anything you need to lay out cash for to get started with. When you first get going, try things that you can start today, tonight, this weekend.

I could go on and on and on for days with stories I have about friends who thought they had to buy a new truck before they could get into this business. Or how they thought they had to buy a new commercial lawn mower before they could cut lawns. Or how they needed a new computer before they started their business. Doing so is a big step in the wrong direction. Once you start thinking like this, you are looking at obstacles. You don't want your list to contain obstacles. Don't tell me you need this new item before you get started because then you are going to tell me next you can't afford it. Since you can't afford it, you won't be able to get into that industry or worse yet, you are actually going to go into debt to buy something you don't need and you won't be able to afford.

Have you ever heard of a book called The E-Myth? (e standing for entrepreneur). If you haven't, please buy it and read it. It's a great book and it will open your eyes to many things. One of the most important issues it discusses is how there are two distinct skill sets one needs to know in order to successfully run a business. The first skill set is knowing how to perform the service. The second skill set is knowing how to run a business which sells that service.

Ok what do I mean by that? Say for instance, you work for a lawn care company and you have learned a thing or two on how to maintain a yard. You know a little about the equipment you need. You know how to operate that equipment. You know how to perform the job. That's great, fine and dandy. But ask yourself what do you know about running such a business? What do you know about marketing the business? What do you know about getting customers? What about making customers happy? How to resolve disputes? How to schedule and bill jobs? Paying the proper taxes? Getting the proper licenses and insurance?

Unless you practice that stuff everyday, you are going to be in for a world of hurt. Many people have quit their jobs and opened a business the very next week only to be out of business shortly after because they didn't know anything about running the business. Most importantly they didn't realize there was a different skill set required. So as you read this now, I want you to say with me, yes I realize there is a different skill set required to run the business I want to run and yes I am going to make it a point to improve my knowledge on this new skill set.

Now that you realize you will be needing to learn a new skill set to run your business, you will see why I am so against you going out and spending your life savings on new equipment. This is equipment you won't know how to market, to get the business to pay for it.

Here is another example to prove my point. I had another friend who worked for a franchised service company. He would often tell me how his boss made sooooo much money. Everyday I would hear how he cleared thousands of dollars a day and how easy it was to do the jobs. Guess what came next. He decided to buy himself the equipment needed to do these jobs. His truck was

$18,000 and the equipment was thousand more. All money he didn't have to spend. In fact his credit was so bad the only way he could get the truck was to have his parents buy it for him and he promised to pay them back.

When he finally had all the equipment in place needed to start his own new business, he quit his job. The next day the phone didn't ring. The next week the phone didn't ring. Neither did it for the rest of the month. He asked how was he going to get new business? What could he do to get the word out that he was in business? He knew how to do the work if he could only find it but he couldn't find it.

Something he failed to realize was the power of the franchise. Many franchises are marketing machines. They realize their value is in standardizing a product or service that can be easily replicated and marketed to attract customers. Without the brand and marketing budgets, most franchises would be worthless. Just having the proper equipment alone isn't going to make people call you.

So did his business last? No. It went under a short time later and he sold all his equipment and his truck to his former employer. He totally failed to realize that knowing how to provide a service and knowing how to run a business that provides such a service, were two separate skill sets.

Are you starting to see what I mean now when I talk about this? To be successful, you are going to have to know how to provide the service and know how to run the business that sells that service. Which leads me to my next point. How do you do that? My answer to that is it takes time and practice.

Remember how your parents used to tell you that you need to learn to walk before you can run? The same thing goes for business. You need to take baby steps. The best way to do this is to start a business small and possibly on the side of a full time job or while you are in school. Learn to deal with the little issues step by step. If you take small steps, you will more likely be able to overcome obstacles which can get in your way. And yes there will be many many obstacles. If you are going to succeed, you are going to have to learn how to weave and bob and negotiate yourself through these pathways.

If you try to scale things up too fast, you may very well find yourself unable to deal with the onslaught of customer problems. So my advice to you is to take things step by step. In the beginning fight your battles one at a time. By going slow you will hopefully be able to resolve one issue before you move on to your next issue. You will learn to see problem customers before they become problems. You will learn, not everyone is a potential customer you want to service. 10% of your customers will use up 90% of your time. You will learn how to let those 10% go and fill them with customers you work better with.

Here goes another example. I had a friend who owned a retail store. He felt people would never try to steal from him. Over time, he got burned on many occasions. As President Ronald Reagan used to say "trust but verify." You can trust people and think the world of them but make sure you have checks in place to verify they stay good and trustworthy. Having these checks will keep us all good and on the right path.

His store had a no refund policy. He felt very good about this policy and thought everyone would simply understand. Well he ran into a customer that didn't understand his point of view. The customer purchased a product and felt it was defective after many months of ownership. He demanded a refund and threatened to sue if a refund was not offered.

The first time you are threatened by a lawsuit it tends to shake you up a bit and keep you up at night waiting for the lawyers to contact you. This did shake him up. So he did what he thought was right, he wrote to the customer and apologized and said he would do anything he could to resolve the issue. The customer's attorney took this as an admission of guilt and used it to sue him with a deceptive trade practice lawsuit. Such a lawsuit would multiply any award won as well as add the additional twist of if convicted of deceptive trade practices, the business owner's insurance would not cover the cost and it would have to come out of his own pocket.

Just as this was going on, another lawsuit popped up with another customer on a similar issue. If he had his return policy advertised in the store for all to see as well as printed on his receipt, he could have avoided all of these problems. This one, two punch almost knocked him out of business. A little research on his part would have shown him that his competitors had return policies written on their receipts and in their stores and he should have seen he needed to do this too. Trust your customers want to have a good relationship with you but verify it by having agreements spelled out for all parties to read and understand.

Being different is great. If you like to be different, I think you will find a lot of success in the business world, but don't be such a rebel that you ignore common business practices. If you do, you are going to set yourself up for failure. Some customers will take your 'kind' policies and beat you over the head with them. Their lawyers will run circles around you with them. Be a rebel but be smart and be profitable. Rebel within the infrastructure that has been provided for you by others who have walked along the path you now follow. Make sure your business policies are similar to other competitors until you really know what you are doing and then you can alter them.

Taking small steps allows you to deal with these problems as they arise and learn from them. After you run into such problems, fix your business and patch things up so you won't make the same mistake again.

All too often our society makes a big fuss over a couple of guys who create a search engine like google or create an online video site like youtube. Business article titles read "two dudes become billionaires over night." Well I am happy and applaud them. Good job guys, but for the rest of us, it's probably not going to happen like that. If you swing for the fence, many times you will find yourself striking out. The problem with striking out in business is that sometimes you only have one shot. You swing, you miss and you give up or your spouse makes you give up or your financial situation makes you give up.

Don't spend cash unless you absolutely need too. Cash is your business' lifeblood. Swinging for the fence by spending all your money on something is a really good way of losing and losing fast. It's like playing Texas hold'em poker and going all in with a bad hand. Instead of this, try going for base hits. Take small swings. Have smaller more easily achievable goals. Go for goals that cost little to no money.

Tell yourself, for instance that you will start a lawn care business and cut 1 lawn per weekend. Get on your computer and print up some business cards. Tell yourself that your goal is to hand out 20 business cards this month. Then try to hand out more in less time. Then try to get more customers. Learn how to deal with customers as you grow at a manageable rate.

If you don't take small steps your chances of success will diminish. Most likely you will find yourself frustrated before you get anywhere. Be smart about things, otherwise you may find yourself in a worse situation than when you started.

Don't jump into the abyss. In one of the Indiana Jones movies, there is this scene where Indy takes this faithful step across the abyss and finds there is a pathway for him to follow. That was fine and it was a great movie, but avoid doing that at all costs. You should be in training to last many rounds in this battle that will be your business. Don't just make one jump into a body of water without knowing how to swim. Start off in the shallow end and go deeper gradually. The longer you have to experiment and learn, the better your chances are of growing over the long haul.

I know the temptation can be great. We have all heard the phrase it takes money to make money. Or you have to spend money to make money, but when you are starting out, don't do it.

Time for another story. I had a friend who wanted to start a restaurant. He worked as a chef at a restaurant and had all these ideas in his head of menus he would make and items he would cook. He was sooooo excited about this. Did he ever run a restaurant? No. Did he know anything about running a restaurant? No.

He found the perfect place and he wanted to spend thousands of dollars getting it to look exactly the way he envisioned it. He signed a multi-year lease. When he finally got the place started, he was broke. He would call me laughing how he had read that one should have at least a year and a half of the money needed to operate a restaurant in the bank as a cushion before one opened a restaurant. He pulled it off with just a few thousand to spare. Well guess what. No customers came. He could have been the greatest chef in the world, but he didn't have any money coming in and was dead in the water.

As he languished there day after day watching his ship sink, the vultures circled. A radio advertising salesmen came knocking on his door. Oh he promised the world. His radio ads were going to bring in soooo many people all for only $500 a month. $500 a month this business owner didn't have.

If you expect such a hail mary pass to save you, the chances are, you are going to sink. These salesmen get a big commission on the sales of ads and most of the time their ad results are terrible. It's the same with cable TV. I don't want to see you in a situation where you are sinking and your last hope is an ad salesman.

What should he have done? Instead of a restaurant, how about starting small with something more within his budget, like a hot dog cart? I found some online for a few thousand dollars. He could have operated one on the weekends or at lunch time if he changed his schedule to working nights. He could have played with this and learned the ropes of running a business. Built up a brand. Built up a customer base. Call it Crazy Johnny's Burgers and Dogs. If he made some tasty hamburgers and hot dogs at a good price, people would come from miles around to buy from him. Then as he got bigger, he could maybe get a truck. Possibly purchased a truck with an oven and made pizza too. Do something different. Experiment. Then he could later open a store front. Take small steps. Give yourself a couple of years. Learn and grow! Experiment, experiment, experiment.

But since he didn't allow himself time to learn and instead spent all his money on one shot, he went out of business. All those business contracts and leases he signed, well guess what, those people still want their money and they sued him. His credit is now in terrible shape and he had to file for bankruptcy.

It's just not worth it! Don't go all in. Improve your odds of survival. Break your journey down into digestible sections.

Ok so say you have been able to get your business up and running for a year or two. The rule of don't go all in still applies. Let me jump to another story to show you what I mean. You never really are ever out of the danger zone. You are always one step away from shear disaster. The best thing you can do is build up cash reserves to do battle when battle is called for.

Now let's move on to a story about my next friend. He started up a small dent repair service on the side. WOW what a great business I thought to get started in. It had very low overhead. I mean what do you need? A suction cup! Well maybe a little more than a suction cup, but you get my point. So he started this business up on the side. He had a full time job as well. Every once in a while a wicked hail storm would come through the area and pummel cars. The cars would end up dented all over. So what do you do when your car is all dented up? You call a dent repair service.

When you called, he would drive over to your house. That allowed him to not have to pay for a shop or have to insure it. He would then use his suction cup and pop out these dents on the spot and most of the time, get paid in cash. The customer was happy. He was happy. Onward he went. Great huh? Well things improved. Word got out and his business grew.

After a year he quit his full time job, rented out a shop and had a big sign out front letting the area know he was there to service their vehicles. He also started to hire a staff to help him work on more cars at a time. Well one day another wicked storm came through and it banged the heck out of a fleet of rental cars. So this rental car company went to the phone book, it found his dent pulling company and made the call.

Oh boy! A fleet of cars! Wow! He hangs up the phone and jumps for joy, his ship has finally come in. So off he goes to the rental car facility. Day after day, week after week, he pulls dents from these cars. Since he had no time to work out of his shop, he closed it down 'temporarily.'

But wait. Doing work for the rental car company was a little different from pulling the dents of his regular customers, he finds. Normally he pulls the dents and he gets paid. He then moves on to the next car. But with the rental car company, he has to pull the dents, submit an invoice and wait at least 60 - 90 days to get paid. At first it didn't seem like a bad idea at all. I mean it was a larger company right? This is how larger companies handle things right? I mean if you want to play with the big boys, you have to be willing to work with them.

Well now he finds he spends all his days there. It's easy work and he even hired a bunch of new employees he had to train. It really seems pretty simple, I mean all he has to do is show up and work on all these cars. There are so many cars it might take him a year to get all the work done. But oh the money he is going to be paid. This is going to be huge! He can already see how he is going to be able to move his wife and children into that bigger house they had their eyes set on.

A funny thing happened though on his way to those big dreams. He had expenses to cover. His employees weren't going to wait to be paid every month. They wanted to be paid every week. If they weren't paid, they were going to walk. So he paid them. He paid them from his savings account. As the months went by, he handed in his invoices. He couldn't believe how much he was billing them for. Oh how incredible this was. He was so excited. His wife was so excited. He never dealt with such an experience before so he lacked the skill set to deal with it properly. When the invoices weren't being paid, the rental car company assured him everything was fine and he would eventually get paid. They told him to look out on the full lot of new cars they had. Of course they had the money! It just takes time to get it from their home office.

When his savings ran out, he took a loan out on his house to cover his living and business expenses. He was starting to get a little nervous now. This wasn't funny anymore. He was digging himself into a hole. The car rental company told him not to worry and to continue repairing the cars. Well he explained that he really needed to get paid and he would have to stop working soon if he didn't get paid.

This is when things took an ugly turn. They told him that they had a deal with him. He was to repair all the cars and if he didn't, he would be breaking their verbal contract and if that were to happen, he wouldn't be paid at all.

Well that's just great. Now what? Now he is sinking, should he push through and finish those cars or should he quit and cut his losses. Well, at the first sign of trouble and trouble being the customer not paying their bill on time, that would have been a good time to stop work until payment was made. Instead he continued along and guess what happened. The rental car company that assured him they had the money to pay him, well they didn't. They had filed for bankruptcy. You know what that meant? It meant most likely, he would never get paid.

What happened to him ultimately you ask? Well, he lost his house. His wife was so angry with him because of all of this that she divorced him. He never got paid for any of his work. Because he fell so far into debt, and since he closed his shop doors for so long he had to get a job to immediately bring in cash flow. What does he do now? He drives a school bus. And if you ask him if he would ever try another business again, he will immediately get mad and tell you how his business ruined his life. The business also ruined his marriage.

This could have all been averted, if he kept his eyes open for warning signs. I have to tell you, for a while there I was just so impressed with him. I mean WOW! Week after week, things seemed to be picking up. Business was getting better and better. His customers loved him. I just couldn't get over that this service could make the money he said it was making! But it all just crashed down to the ground.

Please don't let this happen to you. Remember you are not a bank! You are not in business to loan money. You provide a service in a timely manner and you deserve to be paid in a timely manner. Don't let greed cloud your vision. If you aren't getting paid, then cease working for that client and get a collection agency after that customer to get paid for what you have completed thus far.

Keep this in mind no matter what business you are involved with. Sometimes you can be taken to the cleaners by one large customer, so be wary of that, but other times you can get just as taken by a lot of little customers.

I knew another friend who worked as a mechanic at a mower shop. One day he had gotten into an argument with his boss over something that now seems trivial. The argument turned into a shouting match with his boss and ended with him quitting. Over the years my friend would tell me, how his boss was so dumb. Oh how everyone hated him. The customers thought he was such a jerk. He would never cut anyone a break. Sure he ran his business successfully for the past twenty years but in my friend's eyes, this guy didn't know what he was doing.

So off he went on his own business adventure. He was going to open his own small engine repair shop. He was so confident that it would succeed that he told all his friends they should invest in this business. This is the business to be in he said. His old shop made plenty of money and he felt it was poorly run. If he were to run his own place, it would make him at least double!

He knew a lot of lawn care business owners. He also knew a lot of homeowners because he had worked with them in the past. Another thing he did that he thought would really stick it to his former boss was, he stole a copy of the customer list. He laughed about that. He was really going to show this guy a thing or two. The student was about to become the teacher!

A mile down the road he found a shop with a couple of bays to work on equipment. It didn't have any space to store equipment really so things were going to be cramped. But eh, that was ok he figured. The rent was low and he could always expand later. He got a few thousand post cards printed up and mailed them out to all his contacts. In no time at all he was humming along. I never saw a business just explode like this.

He offered good discounts to his new customers and they came in droves. I visited his shop a few times and you couldn't move! Mowers were piled on top of mowers. It was ridiculous! Well I was amazed, good for him. His rebelliousness really paid off. I was thinking he really seemed to be making some smart moves.

It seemed in no time at all, he was buying a house and getting married. I just can't get over this! What a gold mine! He was so right when he told me this business was the business to be in.

His shop didn't have an office. In fact, he didn't have a computer. He had some parts books but besides that, he felt he didn't need a computer. I thought it was a little strange, but hey he was in charge, this was his baby and he was the boss now. He hired a few employees to pick up and delivery mowers and to help him around the shop. He had this bag of money that he would keep hanging from his side cinched to his belt. I thought it was hilarious because I never saw anyone do that before. When someone paid him, they would pay in cash. He would then open this bag and pull out this huge wad of cash and take payment and make change. He must have had thousands of dollars on him at anytime. That really made him feel good too. He told me how he never had so much cash before in his hands, in his entire life!

Well you know, a funny thing happens when you don't use invoices. You tend to lose track of your money. When you don't keep track of your money, you may think you are making money when you are losing it. When your shop is filled to capacity with mowers awaiting their owners to pick up, you tend to let repaired mowers leave without payment to clear floor space. Then all of a sudden, word gets out, that you are a nice guy and if a customer asks, you can get your mower back without paying if you promise to pay later.

Wow all of a sudden customer after customer asked if they can pay at the end of the month when their invoices got paid. Sure my friend says and he forgets. Then he says sure to more customers and he forgets more. Then he finds himself with mounting bills of his own. His cash roll is shrinking and when he tries to stem the flow of blood, his customers get mad at him. They are amazed they can't walk out with their mowers and pay another day. "Oh dude c'mon!" they would exclaim. "You don't trust that I am good for it? Well then forget you, I am going back to your old shop. At least there I will get some respect."

So one by one his customers left, never to return. They were mad with him because he wouldn't give them free service. Or at least let them put off their payments until months later.

You know where I am going with this story don't you? He went out of business. He also had to sell his house and his new truck and move into an apartment. After asking around for a few months, he found a small mower shop that would take him in and offer him a steady salary.

When I talked to him after all this fell apart, he told me how much he now hated people. How people are such thieves. They totally screwed him and took advantage of him. I felt for him, I really did. But I think he let himself be walked over by his customers. You just can't run your business with a pay whenever you want mentality like this. You can't spend all of your money trying to keep your business a float when you are giving your service away for free.

Don't expect those who owe you money to come back and pay you. It's going to be a struggle to collect once you give them back their equipment. Most mechanic shops know this and that's why they have the customer agree to a mechanic's lien when they bring in their equipment to be serviced. You don't get your equipment back until you pay and if you don't pay within a reasonable period of time the mechanic keeps the equipment to sell off to cover his costs. If you are going to be a rebel, you better get paid or you won't be a rebel for long!

If you want to do things different, fine, great, wonderful, but you better know your business basics first before you go experimenting on a larger scale or you may find yourself in a bad situation.

This ex-business owner is so turned off to business now that he will never try another business again. It is such a shame too because if he had just changed a few things here and there he could really have made it work. In fact I am certain he could make it work if he tried it again and this time used a computer and invoices to track his money. I would not suggest at all walking around with a bag of money at your side. Get a cash register. If you are going to be in business try your very best to project a professional image. If you can't afford a cash register, get a cash box. I really think the 'cash bag' worked against him. His customers all knew he had large amounts of cash in his 'cash bag' so they figured they could talk themselves out of paying and it worked for them.

Don't put yourself out to people so far that you let them burn you. Sometimes if you get burned bad enough you never rebel again. You never try again and that is one of the greatest shames I think there is. Can you imagine how many wonderfully talented people there are out there who have tried to start a business or even ran a business and failed, never to try again? I mean if only they pushed a little further and follow some basic rules of business they could have achieved more success than they ever could have imagined. I do hope by you reading this book you will be able to grow and learn from all these experiences I have to share with you and maybe you will be able to share with me some of your stories in the future so we can all grow.

Be a rebellious attention getter.

I have known many people who started businesses and only thought of marketing after they opened their doors. If you are going to be a rebel and get paid, you better let the world know you are in business.

Most businesses never pay any attention to marketing. Some will make it and some won't. But if you know you can grow by marketing yourself, you would be a fool not too. Why do so many rebel business owners fail to market themselves? Well part of it is they don't know how but probably the bigger reason is that they just don't have the time. They are just swamped from the time they wake up until the time they pass out providing their service. In their eyes, providing their services doesn't include spreading the word.

One of my favorite business rebels is Richard Branson. Richard is an amazing man. He started the Virgin company. Virgin Records, Virgin Airlines, Virgin Cola etc. Maybe you can picture him now? If not, do a quick search and you will find pictures of him performing many stunts all designed to get attention. He got my attention and he probably got your's now too.

If you're going to be a rebel, you better let people know you exist.

Ask yourself what are some really off the wall things you can do to get attention. That really isn't too difficult to do. Maybe think of what the average person would do in any given situation and then do the opposite. Simple huh? Isn't that what being a rebel is all about? Now it doesn't have to be things that make you look like a jackass however, they can work too.

Do you remember the movie Jackass and the MTV show Jackass? Remember Johnny Knoxville the star of the show? He got his start by sending out articles he wrote on testing self defense weapons on himself. One time he put on a bulletproof vest and shot himself with a pistol. He zapped himself with stun guns and wrote about it. Isn't that crazy? I mean that really is being a jackass. But he did something different than what a regular person would do. The articles he wrote were picked up by magazines and then later by MTV.

If you watch the trailer for Jackass the movie near the end, you hear one person saying 'this isn't going to work.' Then Johnny follows with 'it might.' HAHAHHA and boy did it work. The film Jackass cost only $5 million dollars to make and it sold over $65 million dollars in tickets. WOW Rock on Johnny. That is amazing. He certainly is a rebel and he got paid. Why not you too?

Do you have to be that insane to make it? No but it is interesting to see what has worked. Each industry is different and each has it's boundaries of 'acceptability.' Some industries are more straight laced while others are crazy where anything goes. Those who push the boundaries can really make change and bring attention to themselves.

Let's look at the computer industry. Back in 1984 IBM was big blue. It was the suit and tie company which dominated business machines for decades. A start up company was about to rock their world. Apple computer led by the rebel business leader Steve Jobs, used a commercial so monumental it reverberates still today. The year was 1984, the commercial played off the book 1984 and in this dreary, drab and gray world of automatons came this blond woman racing down a runway. Wearing tight red shorts and a white top she was being chased by some future looking police squad. Around she spun and released this hammer into the air that destroyed a huge screen with the image of a talking head blathering to a mindless audience, setting the people free. Setting us all free. 1984 was not going to be like 1984, not with Steve Jobs at the helm and not with Apple computers!

Steve did what no one else did up to that point. He said "hey man, computers aren't just for suit wearing businessmen. They are for all of us." Go out and create, learn and rock and roll! It's no surprise that still to this day Apple enjoys a loyal following.

It makes you think doesn't it? What industry are you in and how can you shake things up? What can you do that will cause a sensation? What can you do to rock the foundation your competitors base everything on? How can you harness the rebel within and get paid? Do something different and get people to talk about you. Get them talking and let the world know you exist and you are in business.

Remember the movie Cannonball Run? Here is a little dialog between two of the characters in the movie.
Batman: Mad Dog, you ARE going to take the shortcut to the Interstate, aren't you?
Mad Dog: We're here to win, ain't we? If you're gonna be a bear, BE A GRIZZLY!
Both: ARRR!

That's right! Be a grizzly! You are only here for a short time and then you will be gone forever so make your presence known.

What's the point in being a rebel if you aren't going to rock like a rebel and get paid? You can do it! Just unleash it! Step by step, up the volume. Each time you try something a little more outrageous, go a little further over the top. Soon, you will find yourself in another sphere, untouchable by your competitors because you will indeed be a rock star in your industry.

Create the business you want.

If you are unhappy with your business, you have only yourself to blame. The same should hold true with life in general. If you are mad about your current situation, stop blaming others. It won't help you resolve your current problem. You have to look inward to find your happiness and direction.

Over the years I have heard many stories from many business owners. I can remember one conversation with a business owner who had been in business over a decade. He told me how it seems tougher and tougher to please people nowadays. Things just haven't gotten easier, the way he had always envisioned they would. The more projects he works on for customers, the more unhappy people he came into contact with and the more he found himself unhappy with his business.

"Is everyone sue happy nowadays?" he asked. I don't know if we can pull up some charts to see if there is more litigation now than a decade ago but what I can see is how an unhappy business owner can bring himself down. I can remember a day when if a customer had an issue with one of his projects, he would gladly work on the project until the customer was satisfied. Now more and more I hear his attitude of "screw' em."

Now come on, really, how far are you going to get with that attitude? If you ever find yourself getting to that point remember it's going to effect your being and it's going to effect your business. If you really don't like being in this business anymore, find something else to do. Be happy. The happier you are, the better you will feel and the better your business will operate.

There are also plenty of things we can all do when running our business to create the business we want. If you do custom work for customers, have drawings signed as being approved by the customer. Involve the customer each step of the way. Use contracts. Minimize the surprises the customer may feel was sprung on them. The more they know up front before they spend a penny, the happier the customer will be and the happier you will be. It's amazing how creating company policies and abiding by them can help us all not trip up on the same problems over and over.

Remember you are the captain of your ship. Not only in business but in life. You have the ability to steer things into positive, happy and healthy directions. The more you get into the habit of making small course corrections as you go the more you will find yourself traveling along the path you want to be on. I think many of all our problems tend to happen when we don't do small course corrections and one day find ourselves being battered by waves against a rocky shoreline. Only then do we start making drastic changes that quite often put us into even worse spots.

When I talk with business dreamers, those who dream of owning a business but have yet to start one, I often hear a common theme. I plan on getting some jobs that will allow me to provide this service. Then I will find someone who will do the work while I run the business and I won't have to work anymore. If you can do this and pull it off, congratulations you are a genius. From my experience it's been such a rarity when this happens, it's almost a fluke.

If you think you will be able to quickly and easily find a service to sell and then hire people to do the service, I think you are going to be in for a rude awakening. More often than not, it simply doesn't work like that. If you go into a business thinking that is the case, you are going to most likely get burned.

Before you can hire anyone else, you need to know your business. You need to know the ins and outs. Any business you want to get off the ground, you are going to have to do it yourself. Remember you can do this, just start small and take baby steps. When you have the infrastructure laid down for others to work within, you can then consider hiring others to help you further your dreams. But always remember as the business owner, you are the leader. Your leadership, energy, focus, and enthusiasm is what will make your business successful, lack thereof will lead to it's demise. If you are into sports, think of yourself as the coach of your team. We all know how important it is to have a positive and enthusiastic coach.

Above all else, be happy! Remember that. Follow that path. Life is too short to be miserable.

Part of being a successful rebel business owner is creating the business of your dreams. That sounds easy but when you think about it, it really can be pretty tough. What is the business of your dreams? How would it differ from what you are doing now? Making a list of these things can really help you in finding your direction. So often rebels don't dream enough of what they want. They seem more focused on simply pushing back against those around them they feel oppressed by. That may be a first step towards finding your happiness but you really have to move forwards from there and come up with ideas that will make you happy.

Getting started.

Don't make it a big deal. How do you get started? Just by starting. Keep it simple. Get some business cards made or make them on your computer and start handing them out to your friends, neighbors and family. Let everyone know you are in business. Knock on your neighbors' doors and offer them your lawn care business services. Do they need lawn cutting, yard cleanup? Ask them how you can help out and then do it.

You don't need any fancy equipment. A simple mower, trimmer and blower will probably do wonders for you. Don't go into debt to get started. Most teens I have talked to usually experiment with trying to find some business and cut some lawns before they go and register a business. When you are ready to take that step, here is some great information on what you need to do.

Now let's look into some of the mechanics of getting a lawn care business started. A Gopher forum member asked this question. "This will be my second year in the business and I want to become legit this year by getting licensed and insured or I will not continue. What do I need to know or do to get on the right track?"

Another Gopher Forum member, Kim responded "Here are some universal things you need to have. First you have got to get a

DBA (doing business as), if you are using any pesticide you will need to get a commercial applicator license, and as for insurance you will need at least limited liability. As for insurance doing residential you can get $500,000 but if doing commercial you will need more (we have clients wanting $2,000,000 coverage). Also a tax id number. Hope this helps you some."

If you have never heard of a dba, as Kim said, it stands for 'doing business as.' It is just you doing business under a fictitious business name. It's like John Smith 'doing business as' John's Lawn Care.

To register your business name you need to go to your local county court house and register your business name with them. This is nothing more than filling out a piece of paper and paying a fee of like $25 or so. Then you get a paper from the county that will be required when you want to open a commercial bank account. You will need a commercial bank account if you want to deposit checks made out to your business name.

Now a more advanced way of registering a business would be to create a corporation S-Corp or an LLC by filing it with the state. I would venture to guess most new lawn care operators just starting up don't do this but if you want to go big and build on a nice and strong foundation, right from the start, this is something to consider.

Mark had another suggestion for our initial question. "Forget the DBA, for $40 more you can become incorporated if you do it yourself, the right way. Also, get commercial auto insurance, it is better and way cheaper. I pay $100 per month per truck for full coverage and the oldest truck I have is a 2000 f350 dump. Also get at least $2 million liability, workers comp, and insurance on all your equipment like mowers, trailers, etc. Hopefully you will never have to make a claim, but if you do, you will be glad you have it. Trust me, I know from experience. I go through Allied Insurance, and I think they go through Nation Wide, which I think might be nationwide (hence the name).

I think I pay around $7 grand a year for $2 million liability, my trucks insurance, workman's comp, snow plowing insurance, street sweeping insurance, and all my equipment. It is well worth it in my opinion."

Steve added "You will not go wrong by having all necessary licenses, permits, and insurance for all aspects of your enterprise. Murphy's law will hunt you down if you don't. It's all money well spent in the long run. It makes you legitimate in the eyes of the customer and gives you peace of mind knowing you are doing everything the right way. Not sure if sole proprietor or LLC, or INC is right for you. A good rule of thumb is once you reach a point when you think you have a lot to lose, tangible and intangible, (like a house etc) look into incorporation in its various incarnations."

How do you choose the right business name for you?

Charlie wrote us and had the following questions about a business name and professionalism.

"If you offer services like lawn maintenance, leaf removal, snow removal, power washing, etc should you stick to name like Charlie's Outdoor Services or GrassMaster Lawn Care?"

Joe suggested "your name should reflect the work you do. So, if you are expanding your services you should advertise a name that indicates you do more that just grass. Nothing drastic - you could even say 'GrassMaster Property Maintenance' instead of 'GrassMaster Lawn Care'. So you're still GrassMaster but on your flyers, invoices and other stationary, you let people know that you offer these other services.

Expanding into other services is a great idea."

Josh asked "I was wondering if you guys thought my business name would hold me back. My target customers are pretty much high end properties, with customers that want superior lawn care (at a superior price). I am planning on doing mass advertising and trying to brand more this year. If this name will hold me back I want to change it now while I barely have anything invested in it. Since I want to brand I am assuming I need to stay away from "lawn care" and such. If you think that my name will hold me back from my target market, please tell me and if you have any ideas let me know."

John answered "Josh, if someone was to come to me to come up with a brand identity package for them and they were branding from the beginning, meaning they had to come up with a name. One of the first things I would ask them is what their target audience was and what aspects of the business of lawn care you offered and if they had any ideas of a name in mind. I have to be honest with you and don't take it the wrong way but if you told me your clients were mainly high end and your idea for a name was GrassMaster I would advise you to look at different ideas for a name. The name kind of says residential lawn care for small to medium clients not high end landscaping for wealthy home owners and large corporations.

Now that being said, if your name was already established and that is how you started and made your business successful using that name I would be hesitant to change it. That would be re-branding and unless you are a household name with lots of money to spend on advertising to have people think of you when they see the new name/logo takes a lot of advertising dollars. Establishing an identity is one of the most important things for a business that wants to grow and become more and more successful it is how you make people think of you when they need your service or product or whatever it is."

Chestin said "when coming up with a name for your business, you definitely want to put some thought into how well it conveys the services you provide, but it's my opinion that a name isn't necessarily going to hurt you IF you have a strong sales message. A lot of businesses invest tons of money (some of the MBA run ones invest millions) to come up with the 'perfect' name, but neglect to put together any type of message that differentiates them in their marketplace. Dumb, dumb, dumb.

As for the name you have currently and whether or not you should stick with it, I most definitely think it's a name you can work with. Whether or not you're working with high end customers or businesses doesn't matter as long as you have a strong sales message that sets you apart.

However, keep in mind that if you decide to stick with your name you might need to be prepared to adjust your marketing message in the future if your services ever change or expand.

For example, what if down the road you find you're getting asked a lot about landscape installations? While you may not do them now, it may be something you could add down the road. If that's a possibility, you'll have to put some extra effort into adjusting your sales message to cover these additional services, but it could definitely be done.

I know this probably doesn't give you the direct answer you're looking for, but you need to decide if you think you have a strong enough sales message and how future changes to your business could impact that message."

Let's look at this a little further.

- **WHAT IS A DBA**

A dba (doing business as) is a certificate you are legally required to file to operate a lawn care business under a fictitious name. It allows you open a business bank account and be legal. But keep in mind, it does not provide protection for your personal assets because the business entity is still a sole owner. You, the sole owner, are still liable for any and all civil or financial liability that the business incurs.

- **WHAT IS A CORPORATION OR LLC**

A lawn care corporation or LLC is a separate and distinct business entity - separate from its shareholders / owners. In such a structure a shareholder's / owner's assets, are not at stake if the corporation is sued and a judgment is entered against it for civil or financial liability.

Only the (corporate or LLC's) assets are at stake. If the corp has one lawn mower and $2,500 in a corporate bank account, that is all that can be seized. If you file a dba and you are sued, you are liable for all business liability.

- **Should you file a dba, Incorporate, or Form an LLC?**

In general, if you are one person with a lot of personal assets, you should incorporate your lawn care business or form an llc. This will provide you with better legal protection. If you don't have too many assets (such as a home and an expensive car), you may want to simply file a dba to start. Filing a corporation, depending on the state you want to incorporate, or form an LLC, may cost $100 to $200 more than a dba but it protects your personal assets. A dba does not protect you. If you file a corporation or an LLC, you don't need a dba.

If you do decide to incorporate, the default type of incorporation is a "C" corporation. Then, you can change it to an "S". Or you can file an LLC. When you get to this point, you should consider talking to an accountant or lawyer to walk you through the process.

- **Should you get an LLC or a Corporation?**

If you are a small lawn care business just starting out, just get an LLC to start. In most cases, you will not be wrong. An "S" corporation is also a good choice. The point now is to get some cheap insurance to protect your personal assets and both of the above are good choices. Later, you can change structure or type of entity.)

Most lawn care operators don't go with the c-corp. If they want to be incorporated they file as an s-corp.

- **LLC or Inc.?**

Doug wrote us and asked "I would like to know what the pros and cons are in running a small business under a fictitious name or my name, with a federal tax i.d. number or my social security number. I'm very unclear about the LLC or Inc. and what others there may be. I apologize for making this such a broad general question, but I'm just trying to get all of the legalities correct and taken care of. Thank you in advance.

Joel responded by saying "Thanks for your question. It is quite a tall order, however, because there are lots of differences between all the possible legal structures for your business. I would recommend doing a little reading & research to fully understand the implications of choosing the structure that you end up choosing. Just to get you started I have provided a few bullet points below on some of the options available but please do a little research and ask your financial advisor for additional advise (regulations may vary from state to state).

Sole Proprietorship

- Easiest and cheapest to set up. Good one to start out with.
- You can use your own name or a fictitious name.
- You personally assume all liability to do with your business
- Lacks tax flexibility

Partnership

- Put everything in writing
- Allow for graceful termination of agreement in the event that things don't go well.
- Otherwise, much the same as proprietorship

Limited Liability Company

- aka LLC or incorporated company
- More difficult and costly to set up and maintain
- Provides some protection against creditors
- There may be tax advantages.

- **More info on becoming an LLC**

Laurie wrote us with a question. She wanted to know about forming a limited liability company (LLC).

Joel said "the question of whether to incorporate your company is a good one. At first glance it may seem to have lots to offer but make sure to investigate the details before making the move - to be sure it's right for you.

As for the 'how' of forming an LLC, I can provide a little direction but you will have to continue your research because the laws differ from state to state. These things are for sure:

- Get professional advice (ie your accountant and/or lawyer) before forming a limited company.

- You will have to either pay a lawyer to get you incorporated ($$ $) in which case they will provide all the forms and advice you need. Or you can probably save some money and fill out the forms yourself. They have 'Incorporate Your Company' kits in my area here and I'll bet they have them for your state too. I have not read this book but I'm familiar with the publisher and can say the book will contain all the info you need to incorporate). Doing it yourself will still cost you some money as the government will charge you a fee to register your limited liability company. As well, remember that there will be an annual fee to stay incorporated.

I hope this helps to steer you in the right direction."

I'd also like to make a mention here on the concept of partnerships and teen lawn care businesses. First off it's important to remember, most partnerships end up being disasters, but they can be a great way to learn especially when you are just starting out.

When you are a teenager and you are looking to start a lawn care business, many times you will find that it's more fun to start it with one of your buddies. You can split up tasks and just enjoy hanging out with your friend(s) while you make money. It's easiest if the partners bring with them their own lawn care equipment so if there is a problem, they can just leave with their equipment. You will also want to figure out ahead of time, if you do split up, how you will split up everything, including your customer base.

It's really important to figure all of this out before you start so if you have a disagreement, you will be able to split the business up and still be friends.

The learning experience you gain from working with a friend will help you through out the rest of your life. You will learn how to work better with people. You will learn how to be diplomatic. How to resolve conflict. You will also learn great business lessons to help you if you decide to branch off on your own one day.

- **S Corp. vs. LLC: Which Structure is Right for Your Business**

Corporations and limited liability companies ("LLCs") are preferred lawn care business structures because, unlike partnerships and sole proprietorships, both offer liability protection. This means that the owner of a lawn care company cannot be held personally responsible for the lawn care company's debts. The personal assets of a lawn care business owner are shielded from the company liabilities.

S corporations and LLCs are similar. They are both "pass-through" entities for tax purposes; the income of these lawn care companies passes through to the business owner and reported on the business owners' personal income tax returns. This eliminates the double taxation incurred by lawn care business owners of a standard corporation, or C corporation.

So to summarize, we could say most lawn care operators start their business as a dba. If you have more assets you need to protect then you might want to consider and llc or an s-corp. You probably don't want to file as a c-corp because your money will be taxed once as corporate income and then taxed again as it is passes to you as personal income.

- **Sales Tax – do you need to collect it?**

Each state is different and each state's laws differ on what you need to collect sales tax on. Some products and some services are taxable. To find out what you need to collect sales tax on, do a search online for your state's website and then look for their taxation section. You can also check with a local accountant. If you do need to collect sales tax, you will need to get a sales tax license from the state before you can collect sales tax. This is no big deal, just another online form and a fee. Once you have a sales tax license, you can collect and pay you sales tax money either monthly or quarterly depending on the level of taxes you collect. This will differ state by state.

- **Do you need a federal employee ID #?**

You will need an EIN if you answer "Yes" to any of the following questions.

- Do you have employees?
- Do you operate your business as a corporation or a partnership?
- Do you file any of these tax returns: Employment, Excise, or Alcohol, Tobacco and Firearms?
- Do you withhold taxes on income, other than wages, paid to a non-resident alien?
- Do you have a Keogh plan?

Are you involved with any of the following types of organizations?

- Trusts, except certain grantor-owned revocable trusts, IRAs, Exempt Organization Business Income Tax Returns
- Estates
- Real estate mortgage investment conduits
- Non-profit organizations
- Farmers' cooperatives
- Plan administrators

More information can be found at the IRS's small business website.

How many lawn care accounts can a 1 man crew maintain.

Jerry wrote and was looking for insight into how many lawn care accounts he could possibly service as a one man show. Jerry asked "for the single person crew, how many lawn care contracts are needed to maintain a healthy income. I was thinking 40. My brother-in-law does good on 25 but he also does a lot of brush hauling and debris as well. I am only doing lawn cutting and trimming with some hedge cutting and gutter cleaning. My average is $25 per lawn cut. I currently only 10 lawns per week.

Andy: "I wouldn't be so worried about the amount of contracts but rather the amount of income, and what you can accomplish within a week by yourself, without working too many hours.

I have 25 lawn care accounts for a monthly gross income of $4,700, and the only help I receive is on Fridays. My buddy helps me all day for $100/week. I could actually accomplish all the work myself, but the help on Fridays is very nice. Most of my accounts are larger complexes, with only a handful of residential customers.

When I first started my lawn care business, I went to every property management company and introduced myself, and started with a few on some smaller projects and worked my way up within the year to larger complexes. I would say 90% of my customers are projects where a previous lawn care service provider was terminated and I was hired in their place.

So if there's any advice I could give out, it would be to make sure you do the little things like pull the weeds and rake the flower beds, oh yeah and keep that grass green, cause these things are what people want and expect, and matter most."

Steve: "How close to your working capacity do you feel you are at? Are you maxed out at 100% or do you feel you still could take on more accounts?"

Andy: "I would say with the help I get on Fridays, I'm at 80% capacity. This includes taking care of a few properties close to my house on Saturdays. I work very fast and efficient and hard. I don't skimp on any detail of the work that needs to be done, which is why I've been fairly successful.

It's funny, I've pulled up to a house to work and see another lawn care guy at a house next door already mowing, with yards of equal size, I'm done and pulling away and this guy is still edging, with blowing down still left. I think some guys assume the longer they are there the better job their doing?? I can also see this same guy doesn't pull the weeds in the landscaping?? Some people out there I guess are just out to make a quick buck, but I'm in it for a lifetime. Even when I can't do the work anymore, I'll hire someone."

Steve: "What do you think contributes to your ability to work faster?"

Andy: "I would basically say speed, I don't dilly-dally around like I see some of these other lawn care guys doing. I get in, get the work done, and get out. I suppose I get into a routine and get a consistent work pattern. I simply go from 1 step to the next without stopping. I guess you could say I'm great at time management."

Chuck: "By not dilly dallying it will save you time but it's your routine that makes the money. In my area, if you edge the lawn before you mow then you'll have compressed moist dirt into the concrete. That takes a lot of time to clean up. Also if you line trim the grass first, you have to trim with both sides of the trimmer head but if you cut first then your only using one side. These are some time saving ideas that have allowed me to out worked up to 3 others at once."

5 simple ways to improve your lawn care business.

When you are trying to get your lawn care business to grow, think of these 5 simple steps you can easily follow.

Bill wrote "I currently have a lawn mowing only operation, and it's worked out very well for me. My travel time is very low and the routes are tight, with a two man crew averaging about 25-28 lawns per day. This works great in my area, however if I tried this where I grew up in in another state, I wouldn't have had a chance. It definitely depends on the market you're in, as well as what rules you set forth to the customer.

I've had absolutely no complaints this year, and most people are on credit card billing. I attribute this to "choosing my customers" rather than them choosing me.

My lawn care business is only mow and go and has been for two years now. I only use postcard advertising hand delivered door to door to gain my customers. We run 21″ commercial push mowers, no trailers, two trimmers and 1 blower. Basically everything is paid for, and with 22 lawns or more per day it's going well. My next step is getting out of the truck and starting another crew. I have learned a great deal from my first year doing this, mostly:

Keep it simple! I decided to narrow my business down and focus on the 5 main things that I needed to focus on and the rest would take care of itself. If you focus on the most important 20% of your business, you will succeed.

The 5 for me were extremely simple:

1) Find a cost effective way to distribute postcards. I always without fail generate 1.2 - 1.8 % landed job rate from my cards. So basically it's a sure bet if 5,000 go out, I'll always get 60 customers or more. How do I distribute the postcards? I'm considering a direct mail route next year, but I do like the door to door as they at least have to hold it in their hand for 20 seconds on the way to the trash.

2) Do quality work! Sounds like a no brainer, but in fact my major competition now here in the area has a huge turn-over of customers from year to year. Although my business method involves somewhat of a revolving door scenario, retention is a key priority now for me. This DOES NOT mean I stray from my guidelines of service however. It's about a win-win situation with your customer.

3) Strive for automation. I've had almost 80% of my new customers sign up online without ever talking to them. There's nothing better than coming home to 15 e-mails of people signing up for service with their credit card ready to go.

4) Answer phones and return emails promptly! While missing calls can possibly cost you a job, make sure your voice mail directs them to #3, your website to sign up. Always leave them with YOU in mind. I currently do not have a phone person, although it's coming up on that very soon. However, with the proper voice mail greeting you can have people signing up anyway. (Provided you convince them with your website)

5) Maintain the equipment. Again, a no brainer, but honestly I was running low on things to make my biz successful while putting it together over the winter so this came to mind for the #5 slot. There's nothing worse than trying to start a trimmer on lawn #15 and it not starting with 8 more lawns to go that day.

I should also say that I pay my help extremely well also, and I only work with people I respect and admire. I am not doing this solely for income, but for personal satisfaction and achievement as well. Therefore, although I do watch P & L and numbers carefully, I would much rather create a successful work environment for everyone in which we all can grow. This has always paid off for me in the long run, as it's universal law and cannot fail."

Great advice we all should consider!

Business loans to get started.

If when you are getting your lawn care business started, you come to a realization that you will need a business loan, consider this advice. One of our lawn care business forum members told us "I did start my business with a loan, but I made sure that it was one that the business could easily pay off."

Steve: "Do you have any advice to others about the process of taking out a loan for your lawn care business. When you should and shouldn't? Also what you would say is one that can be easily paid off. Where to get it from? What should you spend that money on?"

Chris: "First for the process of taking out a loan. If you plan on going to the bank for starting your business make sure you have a solid, well thought out, lawn care business plan. It is not a bad idea to have a professional consultant review your business plan before you go to the bank. This can get pricey, but it can be the difference in you getting a loan or not. When I say make sure your business can easily pay that loan off, you should make sure that your loan payment is no more than 10% of your projected revenue.

You can spend this money on anything you need, but spend it wisely. I used mine on the truck, trailer, tools, and lawn care equipment. I didn't really have any tools before, so I needed those. I had an opportunity to buy the liquidated lawn care businesses equipment from my previous employer, but it was trashed. Therefore I got my own, new lawn care equipment. If you already have resources such as your own tools use them and spend your loan on other things. I already had a laptop, laser jet printer and office supplies from being in college so I have been able to utilize those resources."

Lawn care business insurance.

16 most common business insurance questions:

How often have you had questions about business insurance but just didn't get around to asking your agent. It's possible you are just starting out and don't have insurance yet. As we have found through our investigation on this topic, no one knows better what your insurance needs are than your local insurance agent. Each company's needs are as unique as the services they provide. Each state will also have different insurance requirements of you. Since these questions come up quite often, we decided to compile a list of the most common insurance questions asked by owners of LCOs (Lawn Care Operations) and found a friendly insurance agent, to give us answers.

1. Question: How does an Lawn Care Operator determine which liability policy should be purchased? What percentage of LCO's have the following coverage? $500,000.00, $1,000,000.00 or $2,000,000.00

Answer: Most all carry $2,000,000 the difference in premium is minimal between 1 & 2 million worth of coverage.

2. Question: What is a reasonable rate for a $500,000.00 / $1,000,000 / $2,000,000 liability insurance policy?

Answer: Rates are based either on number of employees or sales. For an operation with 4 employees an approximate premium would be $2,500.

3. Question: How much more on average is a $10 million or $20 million dollar liability policy, what percentage of LCO's have this coverage?

Answer: Most lawn care companies don't carry these high limits.

4. Question: What is the average LCO deductible for liability and theft?

Answer: I recommend carrying deductibles of $1,000

5. Question: How does a LCO's business size effect their liability insurance needs?

Answer: The larger the company the better ability we as insurance agents have to market them and get credits for their insurance.

6. Question: Is it a good idea to get your business liability insurance through your home owner's insurance carrier. Why or why not?

Answer: No, it is better to have your liability insurance separate from your homeowners due to the limits on your homeowners.

7. Question: Does snowplowing effect your insurance needs if so how?

Answer: Yes it will increase rates 8-10%.

8. Question: Does applying pesticide effect your insurance needs if so how? Does using "restricted use pesticides" increase my premiums?

Answer: Yes it increases premiums slightly however if you get into tree spraying it greatly restricts the markets.

9. Question: Does installing sidewalks, ponds or pools effect your insurance needs if so how?

Answer: It only affects rates if you install swimming pools.

10. Question: Does using an ATV in your business effect your insurance needs if so how?

Answer: Not really

11. Question: Does hanging holiday lighting effect your insurance needs if so how?

Answer: No

12. Question: If damage to a customer's property occurs, at what dollar amount is it worth it to file a claim on the damage? How will this effect future rates?

Answer: $1,000. Insurance companies worry about the frequency of claims.

13. Question: If a piece of your equipment is stolen at what dollar amount is it worth it to file a claim on the replacement cost? How will this effect future rates?

Answer: $1,000.

14. Question: Is it advisable if you provide aeration services to have customers sign a liability waiver for buried / non-visible items that might be damaged?

Answer: It helps but most of the times you will still be found responsible for damages.

15. Question: What are the liability pitfalls of using a personal truck to perform commercial duties?

Answer: Your personal insurance can deny any claims if you are in the course of your employment. Also a personal umbrella does not cover business liability.

16. Question: What are the biggest mistakes the average LCO makes when it comes to insurance?

Answer: Not talking an agent and telling the agent what they are doing so, the agent can make sure there are no gaps in coverage.

To sum this up, Gopher Forum member Joel advises the reader to "use experts - For example, speak to an insurance agent and get some prices for the different kinds of insurance there are. As you mentioned you have to insure your vehicle and you must have liability insurance. What about disability insurance, in case you are injured. What about insuring your equipment for theft and/or damage? These are not required but it is worth thinking about. Ask your agent for prices and details (including how much the deductible is)."

Creating a business plan.

Drawing up a plan is a great way to start.

Do you have to create a business plan before you start a business? No you don't. Is it helpful, absolutely. Over the years we have been lucky enough to help many lawn care businesses get started and created many business plans. Let's take a look at one of them here. I feel this example will help by showing you real dollar values. You can then plug in your own financial numbers to help make it as realistic as possible.

Mission Statement:

To provide reliable, affordable, professional lawn care solutions to customers.

Summary of Business:

John's Lawn Solutions is a (Your Town, Your State) based lawn care provider, specializing in high end lawn care. Our reputation will be built from quality service, educated field technicians, professional client relationships, professional image, and honest workmanship. Our goal is to provide clients with the healthy, picturesque, maintenance free lawn they deserve.

Legal Structure:

John's Lawn Solutions is currently set up as a sole proprietorship. I am currently working on forming a Limited Liability Corporation (LLC).

Customer Analysis:

John's Lawn Solutions will be targeting residential homes in mid-to-high income neighborhoods. These neighborhoods range from developments to suburban areas.
Corresponding zip codes for these areas are as follows: (01234).

Most residents in the above zip codes will be targeted as customers. This population consists of new homeowners to established ones, young professionals to retiring ones, as well as college graduates and alumni. If done the correct way, many of these people can be converted to John's Lawn Solution customers.

Competition Analysis:

There are a few main competitors in my area. They range from a one-man operation to multi-crew outfits producing annual numbers from 100 thousand upward per season. Services offered by these companies include lawn care, lawn installation, landscaping, and chemical treatments as well as snow plowing. Through experience and question asking, I have learned what my local market will bare in terms of the above mentioned services. The main strengths of the competition are proper equipment for the job, the ability to hire laborers, and capital for advertising.

The major weaknesses of the competition are uneducated field technicians and management personnel, customer attention lacks, professional image is non-existent, and attention to detail on the job is non-existent. I have become familiar with the previously mentioned through speaking with homeowners and observing first hand the quality of work put forth by these companies.

John's Lawn Solutions has a Turfgrass Scientist on staff that is well educated in all aspects of lawn care. Employees will be well trained and have numerous opportunities for continuing education in the form of conferences, seminars, and other pertinent classes. Customers are and will be treated as people, not numbers or pit-stops. They will be kept informed and educated on the care of their lawn. Newsletters will be sent bi-monthly to all clients to add a personal touch. Collared company shirts, khaki pants, professional proposals and invoices will help promote a professional image. Clean, up-to-date equipment and vehicles will also be a huge factor contributing to the professionalism of John's Lawn Solutions. Since attention to detail is a huge part of John's Lawn Solutions, extra effort will be made while servicing a lawn to ensure garbage is not mowed over; toys are not destroyed, and no blade of grass left uncut.

John's Lawn Solutions will separate itself from the rest by providing reliable, affordable, professional lawn care solutions to customers. Referral programs will also aid in our growth. Discounted rates may apply to customers that show longevity to the company or encourage the use of John's Lawn Solutions to friends, family, and neighbors.

The intentions of the business are to be the top service and quality provider in the area. This will easily be achieved by offering the best in lawn care service. From educated personnel to state-of-the-art equipment to distinguished professionalism, John's Lawn Solutions will rapidly become the leader in service. Quality is as important as the service itself. Through detailed and informative training sessions, personnel will become familiar with procedures in properly detailing a customer's property. Debris will be cleared from driveways and other walkways, garbage will be pick up and removed, all pertinent areas will be serviced to the highest standard of both the homeowner and John's Lawn Solutions leaving a picturesque, maintenance free lawn.

Management:

I have obtained a vast knowledge of turfgrass management skills from 8 years of employment at high end country clubs. During this time, I learned about growing healthy grass, handling million dollar budgets, crew management, and the type of leader I am. This hands-on experience coupled with my baccalaureate degree in Turfgrass Management has provided me with the knowledge to confidently make agronomic decisions, and converse with customers. After speaking with many potential clients as well as existing ones', it has come to my attention that the area is in need of an educated lawn care provider. This will play a huge role in the success of John's Lawn Solutions.

Business Strategy:

Positive national trends that may affect John's Lawn Solutions are the ever-growing desire to live in the United States of America. People from countries worldwide are flocking to the USA at a tremendous rate. All of these people/families may be viewed as potential customers. More and more people are using the Internet for research and shopping needs. With the aid of a company website, there is a greater chance of being recognized both locally and nationally. A professional website will be a huge benefit to our success.

There are also negative trends that may affect John's Lawn Solutions. The unpredictable price of gasoline along with other fluctuating prices such as petroleum based products will cause companies to adjust prices accordingly or absorb the difference.

To take advantage of price fluctuations, John's Lawn Solutions will have a firm Terms and Agreement policy. This will cover any and all likely possibilities such as additional surcharges for the rise in gasoline or other related property maintenance products such as fertilizer and weed control products.

Moving on, there are also positive regional trends that will affect John's Lawn Solutions. The business is based in a continuously expanding demographic area. Northern cities are encroaching from the north while southern cities are moving northward. This means more potential customers on a local basis.

Of course there are negative trends that will affect the business as well. Real estate is in high demand as a result of the aforementioned. Property is expensive as are the homes located on it or to be built. This leaves less money for the homeowner to spend on lawn care. However, most people are compelled to have something as good as or better than the neighbor. For this reason, a high profile lawn care provider such as John's Lawn Solutions will be called to handle the service.

Homeowners want their lawn to look great. More often then not, they lack the time, equipment, knowledge, or desire to do it themselves. For this reason, more and more people are turning to professional outfits to handle such needs. It may be as simple as hanging drywall, fixing a leak, installing a new receptacle, or in our case, lawn care. New homeowners are becoming younger and younger compared to the past. 25-year old professionals are seeking good rate on mortgages for their first home. This means more potential customers. It is the years of the early career when the professional is the most eager which equals more work which equals less time to maintain their lawn which means call John's Lawn Solutions.

Yes, there are also negative trends that will affect the business. More and more people are becoming their own boss by pulling a trailer of maintenance equipment around and cutting grass. You can see them at every red light with chewing tobacco in their mouth. These are the people that will beat your price by ten dollars to gain a customer. What they lack is a clean appearance, professionalism, education, and a desire to grow their operation. John's Lawn Solutions will capitalize on this by upholding a professional image, continuing to become educated in all aspects of business and agronomy, and having a desire to grow the business into something people can rely on.

Labor:

I have started the business employing myself as the only full time employee. As of this November, it will remain the same way entering the next season. I have pain myself just enough to survive while putting the rest back into the business in terms of equipment and advertising.

Hourly wages paid to employees will be $8.75 to $10.50 per hour depending on experience and job title. Foreman may receive as much as $12.50 per hour depending on experience.

Billable hours will be a direct result of early spring advertising as well as word of mouth. The work week should consist of 5 ten-hour mowing days leaving Saturday mornings for maintenance.

Financial:

As of this October, I have invested approximately $12,627.28 in the form of a truck and equipment. I view this as a very small price considering the amount of opportunity it lends. I will be seeking further financial aid from outside lenders and investors.

The monthly fixed expenses are as follows:

Monthly Fixed Expenses

Truck Payment $212.12
Mower Payment $233.15
Truck Insurance $95.00
Cell Phone $85.00

    Sum = $625.27

Monthly operating expenses are as follows:

Monthly Operating Expenses

Gas for Truck $300.00
Gas for Equipment $40.00
Office Supplies $40.00
Advertising $250.00

    Sum = $630.00

Total Expenses = $1,255.27

Advertising:

John's Lawn Solutions will establish a customer base through direct mailings, door hangers, business cards, as well as word of mouth. Company vehicles will present a logo to the viewing public, uniforms will promote through company insignias, a website will cover the Internet shoppers, and our service will keep John's Lawn Solutions in the public eye.

The amount spent on advertising is $114.00 plus per month. The $114.00 covers Yellow Book advertising. Direct mailing will be heavy in the early spring reflecting a cost of close to $1,000.00. This will be done on a bi-weekly basis targeting certain areas more than others. Through research and experience, I have learned it is more beneficial to send mail to one person 6 times versus 6 people 1 time. This is the advertising strategy that will be adopted by John's Lawn Solutions.

Further mailings will be made throughout the growing season to promote the business and special offers such as "Refer a Friend", Newsletters, and Promotions. The volume of the aforementioned will be a direct result of early season success.

Lawn care business startup costs.

If you are looking to start your own lawn care business but are unsure of the kind of costs other lawn care business owners paid to get started up you should consider these thoughts from our friend Sherman.

Sherman: "Well this was the first season of my lawn care business and I have done really well. When I was putting everything in place to get going I had to make a decision on what type of equipment to start with and how much I was going to spend. At this time I was doing handyman work and was wanting to switch to lawn care because housing took such a dive, and so did the work. So after all the research I did this is what I went with:

- A new consumer. Toro zero turn 42″ with a 21hp Kohler ($2400.00)
- A new Echo trimmer ($199.00)
- A used Echo back pack blower ($100.00)
- A used echo edger ($75.00)
- A new Anderson 8×10 trailer ($1050.00)
- Trimmer racks ($69.00)
- Racks welded on ($35.00)
- 2, 5gal gas cans and 2, 2.5gal can ($ 54.00) rakes and ext..
- I had a truck and Insurance ($159.00) down
- $69.00 a month lic (county & city $45.00 & $34.00)

Now I spent $4,220.00 on getting equipped. I ran an ad in the penny saver newspaper that cost me $97.89 for 8 runs (1 month). My web site was built and hosted for ($99.00). I built it myself with some help from the free Gopher lawn care website templates and some help with content from a Gopher forum member (thank you again). Then I had 5,000 door hangers printed ($173.50).

So to get started I have a total of ($4,590.39) invested.

I got started the first of July, well really mid June with 3 of my handy man accounts I cut with a push mower. Anyway all this equipment has done very well, even cut 5 lawn care accounts with the Toro and the grass was 2 ft tall, it held up great.

Well, I now have 58 accounts, 6 annual accounts made all my start up money back and have $3,692 saved towards a new commercial mower that I should have enough for if as planed by mid July next year.

Hope this gives some insight to those thinking of starting up. And again thanks to the Gopher Forum members for all your help. Your help and insight when I was getting started was what got me going in the right direction."

Find a niche and you will find profits.

A great way to find profits is by finding a specialty.

Isn't the lawn care industry great! I mean it has got to be one of the best home based businesses one can start with very low over head. It is fantastic so many teens turn to lawn care as one of their first businesses. With all the greatness about this industry, there is a downside. Competing on price.

What do I mean by competing on price? It's basically when you price a job below the profitable level. When you hand out flyers that say you will cut any lawn for $9.95 regardless of their size. When you don't register your business. When you don't pay taxes. When you don't carry insurance. All these things destroy the industry.

Too many times a new lawn care operator starts cutting lawns and figures the key to success is to undercut everyone. They feel if they can offer a cut rate price they will become an industry leader. Be forewarned, you have set yourself up for burning out and fading away. Don't look at this industry and say to yourself you will be the next Sam Walton, founder of Wal-Mart, and you will become the king of discount law service. Why won't you succeed at this? Because there is always someone who will come in and then undercut you.

As soon as you have a full schedule and figure you will start hiring employees and pay them under the table, you will find your employees stealing your customers and underbidding the lawns you service now. As you try to improve your business and upgrade equipment, your costs will rise. You may have an accident and break a window from a stone thrown from your mower and you will get set back because you have to pay the expense out of pocket. You may be spraying weed killer and be caught by the E.P.A. and heavily fined. The employee you pay under the table may get hurt and sue you.

Please, please don't go down this path. As we have shown you, it's very easy to go legit. You will feel better about it. You won't have to be constantly worried and looking over your shoulder. You will have set the foundation for future growth.

An interesting point we will see is how offering lawn maintenance services is a great way to cast a net and collect many new customers. Then you can offer your niche services as up-sells. It is easier to sell to a current customer than it is to attract a new customer. Now let's discuss moving upwards. Growing, profiting and succeeding in this industry.

One of our Gopher Forum members, Dave said "with residential customers I started off low balling. I was a teen when I started and was scared to ask for higher amounts of money. I was charging $20 or $25 for a lawn that would by myself take me a half an hour. That seemed pretty good to me I was making $50 dollars an hour. I wanted to get an idea of what the bigger companies would charge for a yard the size of mine (medium) to see what the average going rate was. I called a few different companies and was given estimates in the range of $35 to $40. I was charging $20 or $25 for the same size. I quickly realized that not only was I not making what I could make but also with low balling you decrease the value of the trade.

When I first started asking for $35 dollars for a small-mid sized yard I got turned down several times and gained new customers at that price. There is plenty of grass out there. After a while when we had many clients it was ok to get rejected. Don't be afraid of being turned down because it will happen. Once you get over the fear of asking for higher amounts of money from people you will be in a great position and find your income rising!"

Another Gopher Forum member said "To me, if you want to shot for a higher profit margin, you need to either stay small, or do one particular service very, very good. To the point of where people are lining up to receive your high quality and very expensive service. For example, outdoor BBQ's, patios, hardscapes, micro-irrigation, and color displays/plantings."

Jason offered two niche suggestions. "I have been doing irrigation service work for 3 years in addition to lawn care. There is a lot of money in the irrigation service industry, however you do need to know what you are doing. I charge $75.00 an hr. for labor alone. I buy all of my parts from our local parts supplier and mark up all parts used 3x. You do need to have a comprehensive understanding of how a system works and be aware of local laws. Here in in my area you cannot test a back flow (which is part of the typical start-up) unless you have a license and only a licensed plumber can install a back flow.

Irrigation systems require high maintenance and require servicing at least 2-3 times a year. You will encounter broken heads, pipes, clock replacements, etc. quite frequently and this is all great money. I expect to make $700.00 a day for a full day of service work.

In the fall I perform the winterizations at the same $75.00 per hour with a 1 hour minimum. This is also typical in our area. If you have large systems with many zones be sure that you have a compressor that can do the job.

I have also been looking into the organic fertilizations and pesticides and have thought that this may be a good niche to get into. I have heard though that the products are three times more expensive and less than half as effective. Of course someone buying organic would expect to pay more but I do not think it would work well if the results are not comparable to mainstream fertilization programs.

They make organic fertilizers out of a variety of things such as sea weed and kelp, chicken crap, etc. I have never found a selective herbicide for broad leaf weeds though."

Mary offered this "I have been specializing in planting bed maintenance for the past six months and I do okay. I actually wish I could charge more because I do a thorough job. I have had wonderful comments from my customers. The last customer I had actually got me in touch with a lawn maintenance company and he liked my work also. He doesn't do planting bed work so he was going to keep my number in case he gets any calls for that type of work. I will be looking into getting a partner who will do actual lawn work while I can continue to do the planting bed maintenance."

Gary is a lawn care operator who's niche is aeration. He promotes himself as a lawn and gardening specialist, with a focus on lawn aeration.

Gary says "I can get in and out quickly. I can also do core

sampling and soil testing. I'll often do that for free, to find out what the customer needs to make their yard healthier. If they're interested in having the best lawns they can have, that's how I can help. I like to see healthy lawns."

Gary says it averages about $50 to have a lawn aerated, with larger areas negotiable. Although he does have a minimum fee of $20 per lawn.

Gopher Forum member Kurt said "I don't believe in offering every possible service out there, but I believe in allowing yourself to diversify in the services you offer will allow you to bounce out of slow periods and can ultimately keep a more steady income.

In the past, my family owned a pizza shop and we were basically an Italian eatery. We offered pizza as number one but we also had a lot of Italian specialty meals, and on top of that we had the normal "quickie food" (wings, french fries, all types of fried foods, American style sandwiches and subs). I think the biggest problem with that situation was we were too widespread and overhead for the inventory killed us. If we would have just been a pizza shop or just the Italian specialty restaurant I think it would of went a lot better. My proof that the business structure wasn't right, (our's was a a franchise), and the longest owner of one of the shops was us (for 1 year), other than us everyone had to close up in 4-6 months.

I try to diversify my lawn care services but I don't offer everything. I also think it has to do with the area. If only 1 or 2 other companies offering fertilizer spray services, the odds are good that you will be able to get into that area easily. I currently offer mowing as my main income, landscaping, mulch installation, seasonal displays, cleanups, plowing. I'm certified to apply pesticide and fertilizer but I decided not to, I also cut out shrub pruning unless it's for well known existing customers. I've had nothing but bad experience with one time calls for shrub pruning so it was too much of a hassle.

All the guys I talk to around here always say "I want to get out of mowing and do X" X being landscaping, or fertilizing, or strictly lawn installs. But again this area can't handle it, that's why I feel for this area you have to offer a variety of services to keep income up and in case of a drought or too much rain you have other areas to work with.

Here is a good example of this area not handling landscaping solely. The largest company around here, the most well known and professional looking company, with 20 some employee's is now going under. They still seem to be doing fine but a friend works there and said they're trying to get a loan just to pay payroll (I said trying because they probably won't get the loan due to being so far in debt). They do wonderful work, and the owner is known for being a great business man, but he relies solely on landscaping and plowing. That's it. With the current economy doing poorly and then no snow this year, he had no money coming in and he apparently never kept capital in the company's bank account. If he would have offered lawn maintenance, being his name is so great in the area he'd probably have a ton of work there and probably wouldn't be in the situation he's in.

John said "I think that not mowing leaves a lot on the table. I offer several services of which most I sub contract out, mark up for administrative costs (15%) and I get the opportunity to learn and keep and gain customers. I would love to do just irrigation repairs but I know that there will be certain times of the year that there will not be a lot of work.

Most of my customers are commercial and pay an averaged billing all year. That is nice. I know that I have so much income every month coming and try to keep things going. I have learned this year that I am being asked to do a lot of work that I would not normally do, but the profit margin in these jobs is so great that I can not turn them down.

In my area most of the customers (commercial) only want the basic minimum for turf management, (chemical applications). So there is no real money in them for me, two applications per year just doesn't go far. The biggest problem I find is that the larger companies can do the job cheaper than I can purchase the materials. So I sub to them and make the mark up. No one sees the mark up because it is figured in the monthly price.

The same holds true with landscaping. If a customer asks for me to install a patio or deck, I never turn it down. I network with the companies in my area and explain that I do not want them to go in and take my customer. I want them to know that they work and are bidding for me and not my customer. So far I have had no problems."

Tony said "if you want to charge top dollar, yet do things at a low cost to you the business owner, specializing in one service is great. But for the customers that are looking for an all in one service company to handle everything, it's good sometimes to be very broad. I have found out that you can not always charge top dollar for those type of services when grouped all together."

Al says "There are essentially very low barriers of entry into the lawn care business. Anyone who mows lawns or any handyman can become a landscaper. There's infinite competition in the business. The intense competition in the business has generated, even necessitated, specialization. The boom forces specialization. You have to have architects that plan and design something, someone else installs it and a third person maintains it. No one person can do it all."

Joe added "can I be successful doing landscape maintenance without mowing lawns? The answer, in short, is no.

I'm not saying that it couldn't be done. If one were persistent enough I suppose it could happen. However I think it would be very difficult to build a landscape maintenance business without the mainstay of lawn cutting.

Most landscapes have lawns which means if someone hired you they would either have to cut the lawn themselves or hire a different company to cut the lawn. If I were the company they called I probably would not be too happy about the fact that a different company was doing all the other work. As well, the customer will be more inclined to go with a single company because it would probably be much cheaper and definitely more convenient to go with a single company to all the maintenance work, including lawn cutting.

If you were determined to not do any lawns I think your best bet would be to try and get in with a company who just wants to cut lawns and see if you could work out a deal to share your customers.

I do wonder what appeals to other businesses about not offering lawn cutting. There is obviously money to be made cutting lawns and the extras such as fertilizing, aeration and so forth can make you a very handsome profit."

Rich said "I agree with you. There is one company in my area that tried the same thing. They did not last too long before they needed to start landscaping to make ends meet. I am sure it can be done however you would have to specialize in something and be the best at it before future clients would come to you. I lose a lot of business because I do not offer 12 month contracts. We run April – November and we don't touch snow."

Joe went on to say "I think the bottom line is this...

You've surely heard it a hundred times or more:

People buy benefits, not features.

Your great quality is a feature, so the question to ask is... how does it benefit your customer.

For example, do any of these benefits make sense to you:

I offer very thorough planted bed maintenance...

... so your planted beds will be outstanding in the neighborhood
... so your planted beds will look better longer
... so your plants will be healthier and always look their very best
... so you will have to spend less on top dressing and plant replacement in the long run

I'm not sure which of these you could justify but I'm sure you get the picture. If you can show the customer that spending a little more with you will result in more benefits for them than going with an average job, then you will be able to charge more. Ideally you would want to show that you offer better value than the other guy.

So, in short, you can charge more for a really great job but just saying you charge more because you do a better job is not enough, you have to tell the customer exactly what that means for them.

As far as finding more services with better profits I would always say that is a good idea. I have always tried to offer my customers full service. Most will prefer to deal with a single company for all of their landscape maintenance needs and for me it added variety to my day, which I enjoyed. I think hooking up with a partner who likes to do the lawn work or hiring staff to do it are good ideas."

Is aeration a good niche?

Gopher Forum member Andy asked "I actually started my lawn business this year and the longer I've been here the more I've noticed how swamped the market is w/ guys like me and better.

One thing that I do see missing in this market is aerating. I don't think there are any aeration only companies, and the ones that do aerate generally just do it for their accounts. My business is strictly part-time, so I can afford to run an aeration only business, but I need help getting it going and knowing how to manage the multitude of accounts necessary to run a good aeration business.

Joe replied by saying "Have you put together a business plan yet? Remember that lack of planning or poor planning is a leading cause of business failure so you do well to take the crucial step of writing a business plan.

As you develop your business plan, don't just hastily jot down a quick answer. Think about it, investigate, brainstorm with your friends and family. One of the biggest benefits of creating and writing out your business plan is that it will provide stimulus for further creativity. So let your mind wander and visualize your dream. The end result will be a sharper focus, a clear sense of direction and increased determination.

One note: lawn aeration is a great specialty (and can go well with over seeding, lawn renovations and/or rejuvenations) however don't be so quick to write yourself off for maintenance. A swamped market means there is lots of work available and you can stake you claim if you play your cards right... just something to think about. As you develop your plan you will need to decide which way to go."

Andy then said "I have put together a business plan, I spent last fall putting it together with a group of people and then presented it to my business professor and a couple lawn care professionals. One thing I wished I had done was put it together based on aeration only. I am pursuing a career in fire fighting and having this as a part time thing would be good. Yes maintenance is still a possibility, but I think I might just develop my lawn business just enough to hire some students to take care of it so I can have the summers off (won't be for a while though).

What I am curious about is what is the best way to market this niche service. I have a feeling that my city just doesn't have enough awareness of the benefits of aerating, so it could be a tough start. But is there any material out there that would be a good model for the type of advertising I should do and how to word stuff on my advertisements? Also, I have put together a few spreadsheets on how to make this work and what I have found is you need a lot of jobs per season to make it work. How can I manage these accounts effectively, as right now I only have to deal w/ a small number of lawn contracts? Also, what is a good way to get return service each year? There could be a lot of people that just kinda forget about their aeration the next year and don't think to do it again.

Joe responded by saying "Glad to hear that you spent some time putting together a business plan and even got some different eyes on it.

You definitely nailed a couple of the major challenges with a lawn aeration specialty business. First the customers: with maintenance 50 customers will keep you busy all year but with aeration that will last only a couple of weeks. So, yes, you will need to work hard to attract customers. You need to reach a lot of people in your advertising so consider direct mail and/or Yellow Pages, if your budget can afford it. Perhaps more importantly that getting customers is keeping them. That is, impress them (ie exceed expectations) sufficiently so that they keep calling you back. Even if you do impress you will have to remind people to aerate again.

Perhaps sending reminder postcards or even a personal phone call to say you will be in the area? Keep in mind that many aerate twice a year or more. So if you market the benefits of twice a year aeration (spring and fall for example) then you may get some folks that go for it, but for the others aerating just once will seem like 'the bare minimum'.

The other challenge that you also identified is education. Most (80%) of my lawn care marketing material content focuses on educating people about the benefits of aeration. I always use a little diagram showing how the grass and it's roots get thicker. I used to provide people an 'Info Pack' which listed the many benefits of all my services, including aeration."

How much money can a solo lawn care business owner make?

A lot of times a new lawn care business owner will be working solo and wondering what kind of income can they potentially make? How many lawns can the average solo lawn care business owner service? To get some insight we asked our friend on the Gopher Lawn Care Business Forum to share with us some of what they have found as a solo lawn care business operators.

Chuck: "I work by myself. I can get most of my **average $25 per cut lawns done in 20-25 minutes**. Once I have done it a few times & have the lawn under control & "trained" the way I cut it, meaning the grass isn't too long, the trimming never gets out of hand & the edging has been done before so I don't have to dig out the edges of a driveway that have been covered over 2 seasons ago!

I have a few I can mow in about 17 minutes. Here is my lawn care routine. When I arrive on scene I check the time, get out of the truck, mow, weed eat, edge & blow off. Trailer closed ready to roll, back in the truck. I hustle like heck though. I kinda get in a mode like a machine & keep going all day until my mowing list is done. I should say though, I've gotten very used to using a line trimmer to do edging. It's kind of an art form to do it right but it saves lots of time, the machine is in your hand & running already!

I can't really say what profit I'm shooting for per lawn, I've always kinda tracked it by time. When I'm out mowing I shoot to make $35-40 per hour. This is including travel time & my lawn care routes are not as tight as I want them to be. As I go down my lawn care mowing list, I check em off & mark what I made on that lawn today. Keep in mind with my monthly lawn care accounts in the summer, if I get $85 per month & I have to cut it 4 times that month I count it as $21.25 for that cut. Some months I have 5 cuts, so I rely on the per cut accounts to keep that figure up in the summer time.

Last summer I shot for & usually hit **about $225 gross billed per day**. The most I ever did in a day by myself & it happened to be the hottest day of the season (103 deg., 98% humidity, & 106 deg. heat index) was 15 lawns with 4 of them overgrown for a **gross of $650**.

As far as cost per lawn I don't know, If I could do a month with x# of lawns (the same lawns) every week I could figure it out, but it varies a lot I'm sure. The property lot sizes here are 80ft x 125ft = 10,000 sf subtract the average house, garage/driveway and you get about 7,500 sf or lawn. I do have some vacant lots I mow for a customer once a month so they don't get fined by the township. I run a 52" commercial mower. The 1st time I had to remove my mulch kit to do it (which I charged $250 for the 3 lots to knock em down) after that I mow once per month with deck all the way up at 5". I sold it as "field mowing" & let the customer know it wouldn't be perfect, I'd make 1 pass (flying) & keep the township off their back but that I wasn't going to abuse my machine like that (it's not really that bad) for less than $50 / lot. So I go once a month & make $150 in about 45 minutes.

I have heard of a few guys that are $30 to $35+ a lawn in the area I think the majority are priced around me or lower. I understand if you push quality & demand more money there will be some takers & eventually higher overall profits. But that's easier to do once your busy as heck. Raise your prices & don't take any new work unless at a better rate then slowly drop your less profitable accounts as you replace them or get them to raise up too. I average $35 or better per an hour with travel time because I can do a 10,000 sf lawn by myself mowed, trimmed, edged & blown off in 20 minutes."

Steve: "What kind of mower are you using to do this?"

Chuck: "I have a 52″ 23 hp Kohler Yazoo/Kees Mid max series commercial zero turn. Zero turn is the only way to go! Pushing a mower is too tough to do. I won't even take on a lawn that I can't get my mower in (fenced etc.) Not worth my time & uses too much energy on 1 lawn."

Steve: "How do you suggest coming up with a pricing strategy?"

Dave: "My pricing strategy was based off of other companies; I called them to get quotes for my lawn (~2500 sq ft) and came up with a strategy that brought me in below all their prices. I've had a couple friends bring in quotes for their properties as well, just to get a comparison, and I've always come in near or at the bottom.

I guess based on your market you'd have to adjust…I find with all the trimming and blowing added in, my pricing strategy works out to about $35/hour billed (which is what I charge for most other labor).

I mow all by hand with a push mower…I used to take about an hour or so to do a 2,500 sq ft lawn, but I've gotten faster after a couple years of doing it.

I still have the same pricing, but it probably takes me about half an hour or so to do 2,500 sq ft with blowing and trimming/edging."

Shane: "I won't cut anyone's lawn for less than $30.00 a visit and I don't give any price breaks for annual customers unless they pre-pay for service at least a month in advance. I think you could be making a bit more money if you could differentiate yourself from your competition. I am a new company and have no problem doing this.

Here's an example:

> I did a spring cleanup, 16 yards of mulch, trimmed 60' of hedges, planted 18 annuals, 5 perennials, and charged $1,485.00. My profit for this job was around $950.00. How did I do it? I played the game and talked the talk with the customer, made them feel like they had found the very best landscaper in town. Don't get me wrong the job looked great when I was finished but the perception of the customer was far beyond the one man crew (me) that did the job."

Fernando: "I also started with a 22″ 6hp Yamaha push mower, but my blade was Razor/Chef Knife SHARP! With the blades sharpened I could go a little faster. Manually mowing was one of the hardest things I've ever done and I was doing like 5 houses (only 1 day though). At the end of the day, I was done and totally drained.

But then I bought a 32″ commercial walk behind, I love it!

In my area the competition is real tough! I've seen a craiglist ad that said "mowing starting as low as $10/cut" I don't know how they do it either. My cuts go around $30 or $60-$130 a month. So I say that we are around the competitive prices in my area."

I hope this insight helps you compare your business and see how you are doing.

Equipment.

Buy with cash or credit?

A question came up recently on the Gopher Lawn Care Forum where a lawn care business owner asked if he should buy his equipment with cash and remain debt free or buy on credit.

Joel responded by saying "should I buy equipment on credit or remain debt free and if I use credit - should I lease or purchase?

I drew on my own experience and also did some research to provide the following answers to these questions. First, should you use credit.

The short answer is that if you do not have the money to buy all the equipment you need then just buy the essentials. Use some of your profits to gradually build your business, buying more equipment as you need and can afford it. If you don't even have enough for the essentials... wait.

Now to explain that in a bit more detail. There some exceptions which I'll talk about in a minute but for new lawn care business owner, avoid going into too much debt as you start out your business. As part of your planning you have probably come up with a list of the equipment you would like to buy, but what if you cannot afford it all? Break the list down into essentials and 'nice-to-have'. For example a mower and string trimmer are essential whereas an aerator and power hedge trimmers are nice-to-have.

Can you afford the essentials? Can you purchase used equipment and then afford the essentials? If not, my advice is to bide your time, save your money and plan for your grand entry into the market a little later. Not having enough capital to sustain your business, or having poor cash flow are leading reasons for business failure so you would not want to get off on the wrong foot by going over your head in debt.

When should you use credit? You may need to use credit to acquire bigger ticket items such as vehicles, trailers or large commercial mowers. Again, if you are just starting out then, if possible, avoid credit and buy used. If you choose to borrow however, carefully examine the terms of the loan/lease. Know what your break even point is each month - how much cash do you need to cover you overhead. Avoid easy credit, high interest options because you will pay too much in the end. Ask yourself - and ask the dealer - how much does the equipment really cost, after all the interest. The results may surprise you and force you to reconsider your options.

Finally to the question of when to lease and when to purchase. It depends but to help you decide, consider some of the pros and cons to leasing.

Pros

- Leasing is one way to acquire equipment without the need for an initial cash outlay. Usually there is little or no down payment and the monthly payments are less that you would pay for purchasing.

- There are less stringent financial requirements. It is usually easier to obtain financing via a lease than it is with a purchase.

- Leasing provides a better tax advantage because lease payments are an expense and can be written off 100% each month. Compare this to purchasing where your equipment depreciates and hence you can only write off a portion of the equipment cost each year.

- As well, there may be benefits with regard to maintenance. Check with the dealer as to what types of maintenance and warranty there is on the equipment.

Cons

- Leasing costs more in the long run if you choose to buy the equipment.

- You never own the equipment so you cannot use it for collateral or list it as an asset on your books. If you decide not to buy it then you must return it after the lease term is up.

- Leases are often non-cancelable. If you get into trouble, you may be in an very unfortunate and costly situation.

Weigh the options carefully when leasing or using credit. Read the small print and get legal advice before signing long term agreements."

Equipment advice from a 15 year old lawn care business owner.

Here is some advice on equipment and business from one of our Gopher Forum members who is 15 years old. He has given us some great insight after ending his first full season running his lawn care business. He isn't yet old enough to drive so a family member helps him by driving his truck from job to job. I do hope this story inspires other teens to think big.

Mitch: "I want to update you guys on what I've been up to this year. Things have gone great! Gross profit is over three times what it was last year. I ended mowing this year with about 40 weekly mowing customers. I have an employee, a retired gentleman who is a very hard worker.

> I added a few new pieces of equipment:
> Toro Pro-Line 21″
> Lesco 48″ WB
> Lesco 32″ WB
> Rice 7×16 Trailer
> Billy Goat Leaf Vacuum

I traded my old 60″ ZTR for a commercial 48″ walk behind. It really was overkill for most of the yards I was putting it on, and the 48″ walk behind is perfect! I do plan on adding another ZTR next year.

I really took a liking to my new mower and my dealer support is tremendous! So I bought a 32″ walk behind as well. I have a lot of gated properties, where the 48″ doesn't fit, and this takes care of that! I got it on sale, at one heck of a price.

My old push mower basically fell apart on me. The wheels started coming off the frame, and it was a mess. So I got a professional grade mower and have had no regrets.

I found a trailer online and got it in September. I don't know how I got by without it! It's awesome to have space to spare! I do still have the old 5×10 trailer for aerating, landscaping, etc.

The truck is doing great. It has just under 115k miles, with no major problems. I will be getting a snowplow next year.

> Next Year's Equipment List:
> 48 or 54″ ZTR
> STIHL KM 110 Multi-Task
> Western Plow"

Steve: "Great job this year! What lessons have you learned so far this year that you can share with others just getting started out?"

Mitch: "There are a ton of things I have learned. This year was an eye-opener for me. I was busy all year, never struggling to get lawn care work. I really worked myself hard this year, but it is all paying off.

1. Develop Relationships. I got to meet the owner of the biggest nursery/supply yard around here. He started out just like I am. I do all my plant purchases there, etc. I walked in one Saturday afternoon, very close to their closing time, and I really needed a delivery. They took care of it. I will never forget that, because they came through for me, so I could get this job done. That means a lot to me, and it's how I like to treat people.

2. As Forrest Gump says, $hit happens. Don't get frustrated. I had a day where I blew a trailer tire on the side of a major highway and had no spare. Then I missed my exit getting back into town, had to drive an extra twenty minutes, then had to go back to school, get my school schedule, drive back to the town, then back to the landscape supply shop where I started my day off at. I traveled 150 miles that day. I had an employee on the clock, etc. It sucked, but it could have been worst.

3. Learn from your mistakes.

Mistakes I made:

Not asking for help when I needed it. Especially in the spring, I was working myself to death.

Buying used equipment. I don't plan on buying used mowers anymore. With new stuff, you get a warranty, and a little more power at the dealerships.

4. Marketing: Word of mouth. That's how I have expanded my lawn care business. Truck/trailer signs are great for getting noticed as well. Yard signs work great as well. Even for small jobs (ex. bush/hedge trimming job, stick the sign in the yard while you are there, take it with you when you go).

5. Being professional. I have shirts, hoodies, windbreakers, all with my logo on the back. I've been walking out of the hardware store and gotten people to ask me about work. I always have jeans on when I'm mowing, shirt always tucked in. Safety equipment: Ear muffs (with the radio of course), glasses, gloves, etc.

You have to show people you are serious, then they will take you seriously. Most people don't realize I'm just fifteen years old. I normally tell them after we have discussed work and such. Most people are just impressed and willing to support me."

Be careful not to buy too much lawn care equipment when you start.

Starting a new lawn care business is tough. Make it easier on yourself by giving yourself the gift of time to make mistakes and learn from them. The easiest way to do this is by minimizing your expenses and not buying lawn care equipment you don't need.

Chuck: "I hated my start up time when I was using junk equipment. So I worked hard to grow my business fast so I could upgrade.

But still, it's sound advice. Most start-ups don't make it for very long. So why get stuck with $20,000+ in gear just to realize this isn't for you?
Start small, Baby steps.... "

Steve: "What is your view on aerators? Do you own one or rent one or not perform this service at all.

At what point would you suggest a lawn care business owner purchase one?"

Brandon: "I never have even had a request for aerating. I think if I was going to do something like that, I would plan in advance and schedule a day where I could set up 20 or so jobs to do and rent one. I think that is the only way you can make it profitable."

Chuck: "I do not own an aerator, I think to the right clients it's a valuable service but to most down here they don't care. Our soil here is mostly sand with high acidity... the ground doesn't really "pack" like it does up north. The only people with nice lawns here spend an average $100/month on lawn cutting + $60/month on fertilizer & pest control services + the water bill for properly irrigating..... Most are not spending in the $200/month range on lawn care alone right now. I haven't pushed aerating & really haven't done much fertilizer either... a lot of em don't care as long as their yard is green even with lots of weeds instead of grass.... & cut to look pretty good."

A quick way to calculate the cost per hour of operating your equipment.

When you are trying to estimate a lawn care job, you need to know which equipment you will be using and how much it costs you to operate that equipment per hour. These calculations will give you a bare bones figure. You might also want to include the lifespan of each piece of equipment, by figuring out how long the piece of equipment can be used for in total and how much it will cost you to replace it.

Howard wrote in the Gopher Lawn Care Business Forum "I'm wondering if there is a good way to calculate how much it costs you to run your mower, blower, etc (any gas powered equipment). That way you can calculate how much your actually making on the job."

Sherman: "There are many different ways to figure it out, and many might not agree with my method, but it works for me and if there is a better way, then I am all ears.

Anyhow what I do is this:

> **1st/** figure out how many hours each piece of equipment will run per tank of fuel. (your total hours times your average fuel cost) = run time cost

> **2nd/** figure out your maintenance cost for each piece of equipment. I do this based on a weeks worth of work. Blades, line, oil x 1.25 x total used = total maintenance cost for the week

Add these 2 figures then divide by total run hours and you have your cost per hour. Then add in your man hours cost, this is what it cost you per week to run.

Now add the income of all your accounts for the week, divide this # by the total # of hours run and the difference is your profit or lost."

Choosing the right snow plow for your lawn care business.

If you are looking to add on additional services to your lawn care business to help get you through the winter months why not consider offering snow plowing?

When you are looking for a snow plow there are many different options to consider. Here is some advice from the members at the Gopher Forum.

Rob suggested "I run a Meyers 8.5′ and it weighs in about 880 lbs with mount. You should always go with a wider plow.

1. The minimum plow width should be wider than your tires so you can get traction and you don't pack the snow which allows for easier removal.

2. The wider the snow plow the more snow removed, less time at property = more money.

3. Before the snow hits, you need to do a layout for the property so you know where the obstacles are and how you will attack the drive. You need to know where the snow will be piled and most important of all, will the snow plow fit. The manufactures will only offer one maybe 2 sizes bigger than the vehicle it was designed for. Take mine for instance 2001 Chevy 3500 hd 1 ton dually, Meyers offered 7.5 ft width (smaller than my rear duals), 8, 8.5 and 9ft. I chose the 8.5ft width because of some driveways I am doing, but if I add wings I gain a additional 24″

making the plow 10′4″ so I can plow the K-mart parking lot quicker."

Steve: If you have a smaller truck, you won't be able to mount such a large snow plow on the front of it. So snow plow manufacturers have come up with smaller light weight snow plows. Some of these lighter snow plows come with the ability to apply downward force. You may be wondering what the benefit of this is. I asked what are the benefits of downward pressure for plows on smaller vehicles?

Tom: "You have the ability to back drag drive way. With the lighter plow (350 lbs) you need the down pressure to help. This is very beneficial when you want to drag snow away from the end of a driveway that meets up with a garage door."

What's better, an open or enclosed landscape trailer?

When most landscapers start up their business, they tend to start with a truck only. Later they may add an open trailer. At a certain point you may be asking yourself what's better to have, an open or enclosed trailer and why?

That's the question one of our new forum members asked and he got quite a few responses I think will help you make up your mind as well.

Brandon: "Hi everyone my name is Brandon and I am the president of my own landscape & maintenance corp. I have been in business for 9 years and hope to find continued success long into the future. I was wondering if anyone could provide me with some positive and negative attributes of an enclosed trailer as opposed to an open utility trailer to move lawn care equipment from job to job? I have an open trailer now and I am thinking of making the switch over to an enclosed one."

Keith: I can think of a few pros and cons of the top of my head.

Pros:

- Ability to lock.
- Protection from rain.
- Larger area to put name/logo/phone number.
- Looks more professional.
- Possible increased slipstreaming giving better gas mileage (offset by weight, I'm sure).

- Ability to put shelves/storage areas.
- Protects cargo from rocks kicked up by your truck.
- Winter storage.

Cons:

- Increased cost.
- Increased axle and tongue weight.
- Inability to load from top (leaves, mulch, dirt). This is the biggest negative I can think of.
- Doesn't air out well when mower has wet grass or fuel fumes.
- Reduced freedom of movement when you are quickly grabbing a trimmer, etc.

Chuck: "I run enclosed trailers currently. It is added weight, & it's like dragging an 8' wall behind you so fuel economy suffers a bit. But I think the added security, & having a huge billboard behind you all day offsets the negatives.

I have gone to many estimates & when I pull up they say "Oh yeah, I've seen you guys all over town… you stay pretty busy huh?" The fact that they recognize the rig & that I've been around a while adds instant credibility.

So many guys run trucks with no decals or only little magnets & open trailers. I pass them all day long & they all look the same. So that seems to make a big difference.

The biggest negative I have found is that here in my state, it's damn hot. So when we run these machines for 8-11 minutes at a time & load them up, drive 2 minutes & repeat all day… they don't really get to cool down. An open trailer would at least let air blow past them. I have offset this by running full synthetic oil in all my mowers to add some protection against the added heat & we usually end up throwing the trimmers in the back of the trucks between jobs.

I will stay with enclosed trailers & if not I would have my truck professionally wrapped to make it more recognizable."

I think this decision ultimately depends on where you currently store your trailer. If you park your trailer on your driveway at home and need to unload all of your equipment each night into a garage, that is going to take a big bite of time to load it in the morning and unload it at night. So consider these all of these factors. Constantly strive to make your business more streamlined and profitable.

Are leaf sweepers a good option for professional landscapers?

Are you looking for another way to pick up leaves from lawns you service during the fall? One of our forum members made a post and asked "Anybody using lawn sweepers to pick up leaves? I'm thinking that in some situations, this may the faster way to pick them up as well as other junk from lawns and parking areas.

From what I can find out so far, Parker seems to be the best built sweeper out there, but its a bit pricey and only 36″ wide. I suppose you get what you pay for. Also looking at the Craftsman 46″ wide model. It's half the money with a higher brush speed compared to others. Reviews seem to be mixed on durability.

I'll be using my ATV to pull it around as it is faster than my mower as well as more fuel stingy.

My lawn mower has a 61 inch deck with a bagging system, but it's not that great at sucking up leaves in some situations. The problem is the ground is not that smooth at one particular account and I can't get the deck low enough without scalping and gouging the ground with the deck or blower. Of course that's where most of the leaves are.

So maybe a 36 inch wide lawn sweeper would do a better job in that situation. I can rent one for about $30 for a day. I've been looking for something online and close by. I really don't want to travel too far to get one.

I'll probably just rent one for a couple of days, at least then I will know if it was the right tool for the job."

Luke: "There is a guy in town that uses a self propelled leaf vacuum. The parking lots and the sidewalks are kept free from dust dirt and garbage. He just walks behind the vacuum and sucks up stuff off the sidewalks and along the curbs so the drains don't get clogged."

Andy: "The one by far that's the best I've ever used, the multi-vac by Billy Goat. I got a demo unit from my local power equipment store, this will even pick up beer bottles and not break them, very nice machine."

Justin: "I had a generic tow behind leaf sweepers before and it was a piece of junk. The wheel that turns the sweeper kept getting jammed up and the sweeper ended up breaking since it wasn't turning and I was still pulling it. Maybe there are better ones out there but I wouldn't recommend it to any professional landscaper."

Keep all this in mind when you are considering your options for picking up leaves in the fall.

How best to use a mower vac to clean up leaves and how to charge for it.

How best to use a mower vac to clean up leaves and how to charge for it. Jeremy wrote in "I'm planning on purchasing an ultra vac for my zero turn lawn mower to do leaf cleanup, but I'm not sure how best to use it or how to charge my lawn care customers? Any suggestions?

I've never used the vac system on a rider mower, and my first idea was to just charge them for another cut since I would be going over it more than once.

Example: I have to go over a lawn three times in order to have it cut and the leaves removed. The lawn is $25 dollars a cut so I charge $75 dollar for the job.

Does this sound like a good idea to anyone else, or should I rethink this."

Ken: "I've used a "vacuum" on a zero-turn mower method for a few years now. I've never been able to do a job for only 3 times the mowing price. My minimum is $200 and I get anywhere from 7-11 times the mowing price. I make an exception if we do a multi-stage cleanup. Keep in mind, in my area we often have 4-8 inches solid leaves - completely mulched, one 20k job can fill a 8 x 12 landscaping trailer with four foot sides, but we average 3-5 jobs per trailer load. We use one trailer for towing the mower and one for leaves.

We estimate mulch and cleanups based on mowing price … it's not perfect, but we analyzed all our mulch and cleanups and discovered that we COULD use mowing price as a fairly accurate multiplier, simply because mowing price is based, in part, on square footage of the yard."

Jeremy: "I have not purchased the vacuum yet and don't really know what to expect. What I'm looking to do is to cut the grass with the leaves on top and then go back over it with the vacuum to get all the remaining clippings? Is this a good idea, or do you have a better recommendation? I just want to be the most efficient I can be, but really have no experience. Any advice would be useful!"

Ken: "I'm not sure about the "cut first / suck later" strategy. I can't say I've actually tried and timed it vs. the "suck from the beginning" method, but I think that simply vacuuming the leaves off the lawn right from the beginning is best, because the grass is standing up and "presenting" the leaves to you ... and they're still in one piece and light. If you mow first, you sort of "drive" everything into the ground, then you're picking up much finer, heavier particles. You want BIG AND LIGHT vs. small and wet and heavy for your vacuuming system.

What we have found works for HEAVY leaves is to go over them once with the deck completely raised, which will suck the top layer without chopping and mulching the grass up too much ... then we lower the deck and repeat as needed.

We have also found that sometimes it's better to just shut the z mower off, and do a "very quick and dirty" blowing of the bulk of the leaves into a pile and tarp them into the woods. This is ONLY if there's ankle deep leaves - which we DO HAVE in our area, or if the leaves are plentiful and wet.

The best of both worlds of course is to have a truck leaf sucker too, so you use that for the big piles of leaves and the Z for the less "leaf populated" areas.

I have found a sub-contractor that got out of the lawn mowing business to concentrate on leaf pickup and hydro seeding, so we're going to use him this year for sucking some of our larger accounts. Very synergistic - using the right tool for the job."

How long should a commercial lawn mower last?

How long should a commercial mower last? This is a very good and important question when you are considering buying one. Here is a great discussion from the Gopher Lawn Care Forum I wanted to share with you on this topic. Keep in mind as you read this, many consumer lawn mowers will only last 200 hours.

Tommy: "I'm in my 3rd season as a lawn care professional. I have around 150 accounts some big and some small. The equipment I use is 52″ walk behind (with 700hrs on it) 44″ walk behind (with 1,300hrs), and another 32″ walk behind. I just got a couple of big accounts and I need to get some bigger mowers. I need to know if it is best to buy new or used? I would like to finance these, so that I can write this off on my business. Any ideas on the finance part?"

Tim: "If you want to write it off, lease for 3 yrs then buy it out."

Tommy: "Thanks. I did not know that you could lease mowers. Is that really a good idea? I'm pretty hard on the mowers"

Tim: "Yes you can, and if your lawn care equipment isn't giving you at least 6 years of service then you really need to take better care of it or you're only costing yourself money. I don't mean to sound harsh but that is just how it is. If my guys misuse or abuse equipment and I can prove it (and I normally can) then they pay for the repairs or replacement of that equipment.

> **ex**. one guy threw a $300 trimmer in the back of the truck and broke the housing and throttle, he paid for it and I kept the trimmer it was only a month old.

That equipment is your bread and butter."

Tommy: "Thanks, How many hours does a lawn mower typically have when it's on its death bed. When I mean that I am hard on my mowers. I mean 10-12 hrs per day 6-7 days a week during the summer months I run these lawn mowers. I do routine maintenance on them."

Tim: "It should be about 5,600 hours but in reality it is about 2/3rds that, maybe 3,700 hours."

Clive: "I came across a mower online in my local area and it has 3,000 hrs. Is that a lot for a diesel mower? I know it is for a gas machine but I don't know."

Tim: "I would have to say it is very close to rebuild time. As you know commercial a gas engine will last about 2,100 before you replace or rebuild and that depends on how it is taken care of, proper maintenance is the key. A diesel engine will last about 2 times what gas will if it is taken care of and serviced properly.

So if it has 3,000 hrs and life expectancy is only 4,000 then it is close. If the price is right and the deck is still in good shape, by this I mean (no welds and good pulleys and bearings and not much work is needed) then it's up to you at that point. If it is a Kubota engine then you may (depends again on care of the machine) get about 5,000 hrs and then you're still over half way to rebuild time.

Remember that diesel machines take more maintenance all the way around."

How to price and estimates jobs.

How to price jobs in order to make a profit.

Correctly pricing your jobs is very important. It wasn't too long ago on the forum we were talking about an LCO who built his company up to a $400,000 a year business. When he was making $100,000 a year, he thought that if he could make $400,000 he would also multiple his profits by 4. But he ended up losing money and his company almost went belly up.

He later hired a consultant and found that he wasn't pricing his jobs evenly. The larger the jobs he had, the more money he lost on them. It wasn't until he reviewed all his jobs that he found out where he was losing money. Then he raised his prices. His big fear was he would drive his customers away, but only 10% left. That was the 10% of customers he was losing money from!

Something to think about!

Dan asked the following question "I currently provide janitorial services for a number of accounts. They have approached me to bid on their lawn care and snow removal. I have a son who has cut residential lawns for a few years but to bid on larger accounts with snow removal is foreign to me. Are there formulas I can go by and where can I get your book? Thanks for helping out a rookie."

Joel said "You must be doing great work on the inside of the building for your customers to ask you to look after the outside too. Well done!

If your son has been cutting residential lawns for a few years, he is probably ready to make the leap into larger commercial contracts. They are a different breed than residential but often times well worth getting into. There are guidelines, principles and formulas that can help when pricing these types of jobs (or any jobs really). Unfortunately, there is really no magic formula that will spit out a reliable number for you though."

One of the things we have seen in the past on the Gopher Lawn Care Business Forum when lawn care business owners are making the jump from residential to commercial is they tend to underbid themselves. To overcome this, the lawn care business owner could consider actually mowing the property for free to get a feel for how long it would take and see what is really involved. I know someone reading this might say, "I am not going to give anything away for free," but the flip side is this. You aren't giving away anything for free, they are giving you an opportunity to learn and grow. If you bid the job and sign a contract for a year and then later find out you underbid, it can really put your business under.

Why put yourself at such a risk, if you can easily take a few hours to learn, experiment and grow.

Joel replied "That's a good point. It would be tragic to sign a contract and then realize you underbid. A free cut is a small investment. Of course, once you have some experience in commercial you will be able to bid them almost as easily as you do residential. On the other hand, the free cut may also build goodwill in your company so it may be something you want to continue doing with new clients."

Some things to keep in mind are, always try to minimize your downside. Take everything step by step and help your business live another day. The longer you are in business the better educated and prepared you will become to deal with situations that present themselves. Don't get too excited over anything where you jump and fail to think things through before hand. Sometimes one error can sink the ship.

Kurtis had this to say. "First thing you always want to do is actually walk the property and don't be in a rush to get in and out of the estimate. I did this once and when I got there I was in for a surprise. I didn't know there were four ditches in the front lot that would need trimmed and gone around while mowing. Luckily for me it still took the estimated time that I figured and my price still worked out to what I wanted.

What I do when estimating large properties is I figure out how long it's going to take me. Break it down into smaller sections if you have to. Then I figure my hourly rate or what I want to make from the property and put a price together from that. A lot of times commercial properties are going to be broken up into a few mowing areas, I find it easier to just figure out the time it will take for each and then figure out the total time plus drive time."

John asked "I am just starting my business up this year. I have done a lot of work with well know professionals in the area, but I am still young. I somehow think people will not trust my estimations to be the best, what can I do about this?"

Joel replied "this is a great question. It can be a challenge for a young person to be taken seriously in business since you lack the experience of other more seasoned companies and even if you have experience, you may not be taken seriously. It boils down to confidence. If your prospects detect a lack of confidence in you this will likely scare them away. You don't want phony confidence either though. Most people can see right through this eventually. The best way to built confidence is through learning.

You need knowledge to show real confidence so keep learning and make sure all your customers know that you are an expert in this field. It seems you are on the right track - you have mentioned that you have some experience working with professionals - so let your customers know that. You can mention it specifically (I have x years in the business) but more importantly show them you are experienced in the way you operate your business.

Be professional. Show up when you are expected, dress smartly (company shirt?), have a professional attitude, have a clean truck, make sure your marketing material says 'I'm professional'. As well, use your knowledge about the industry when talking to customers. Don't point and talk about 'that bush'. Use the name of the shrub. Explain things like when to water the lawn, when to fertilize, how to make the lawn look the best. Basically let them know that you are knowledgeable in this field and this will speak volumes no matter how young you are."

Charge by square foot or man hour?

Randy wrote us and asked "How should I bid on jobs? Do it by foot or by man hour?

Joel said "In short - you should definitely have an hourly rate but avoid using it. You want to quote quality - not time. In other words it's better to say "I'll perform these set of services, to your satisfaction, for $50" than to say "I'll spend an hour at your house for $50." Of course, you can use your hourly rate to base your price on but we don't need to pass those pricing details on to the customer. We don't need people watching the clock and as you get better at your job and shave a few minutes off of it - that should be to your advantage.

Many jobs, such as fertilizers and over seeding, I quoted per 1,000 square feet. Others I based on an hourly rate but did not tell the customer it was based on time.

I do not believe there is a set rule to cover all situations but I hope these guidelines help."

Should I charge for estimates?

A question came in if a lawn care business owner should charge for estimates. Either $5 or $10.00 to cover gas. Then if the customer goes with you, they will be credited in their first bill.

I don't think you should charge for estimates because the estimate is your chance to sell your services. A potential customer is going to want a few estimates and if the others are free, they will go with another lawn care business. If you can't get to the point of selling your services, you are dead in the water.

In fact, it would be wild if you would tell the customer you will pay them to give them an estimate which would be credited on their first service.

Joel said "I could not agree more. I think it would be a mistake to charge for estimates and you would probably find that you don't get as many estimates, which means less opportunities to sell your services. On site visits are your chance to impress prospective customers and win their business, which over the years can add up to a lot. As well, you can upsell additional services while you are there. I say get every estimate you can!"

What is the best way to bid an apartment or condo complex?

A Gopher Forum member was looking into jumping from residential to the commercial lawn care market and wanted to know the best way to create a bid for commercial properties.

Joel said "this question is one that many have as they get ready to break out of the residential market and into commercial/condos.

As you might have guessed there is no easy answer or magic formula that will produce a bid on larger multi-dwelling properties. Experience is key, which is why getting a year or two under your belt doing residential is advisable. After that, you should be very competent at bidding and doing residential jobs and the same principles will help you bid the bigger properties.

There are a couple of methods you can try as you bid on these properties. Both require breaking the job down into smaller, easy-to-handle portions.

The first is to estimate the time it takes to do all the different jobs and then add up your time over the year. For example, if you think it will take 3 hours to cut and edge the lawn, then multiply this 3 hours by the number of times you expect to cut the lawn. Add on the time it takes to do other tasks such as trimming, pruning, bed care, fertilizing, general clean-up, blowing off and so on. Don't forget anything! Create a worksheet you can use that lists all the jobs and figure out how long each will take. Once you have your total time for the year, you can multiply by your hourly rate. Don't forget to add on materials and equipment overhead. As well, if your hourly rate does not include general overhead then you should add this on to the total as well.

When you supply the quote show the cost as an annual fee and broken down. For example, after listing all the services you intend to supply say: The cost of this year-round maintenance program will be $4685/year or $390.41/month over 12 months. (Or something like this).

Another method is to use formulas. This might require a little more experience because it is important that your formulas are accurate. Remember, your quote will only be as accurate as your formulas. However, if you are confident with your pricing you can create formulas like:

Cost per 1000 square feet to cut lawn
Cost per 1000 square feet to fertilize lawn
Cost per linear square foot to trim a hedge

You get the idea? You'll have to measure everything accurately but once you get some good formulas the job gets pretty easy. Of course, you may need to make adjustments (the cost to cut a heavy slope would be more than a flat lawn) so you will have to use your judgment.

You may find that using a combination of both methods works for you."

How to price retaining walls?

Our friend and forum member Tony had asked, "For those who don't know, I am based out of Northeast and our delivery rates have really gone up. I actually just got asked to put in a segmental retainer wall, for a client. When I price a wall, I go by the cost to deliver all the materials, and then I figure in labor. However 90% of the competition just prices by the square foot, in between $20-$30 dollars per square foot for walls. Just to stay competitive, what is the going rate now on walls? Is it still in that same margin, or have people increased that due to cost of doing business these days. I always like to compare, and I compared the price I came up with for this wall with just doing $25 per square foot and they were drastically different. As a matter of fact at $25 per sq. ft., the job wouldn't even be worth it. It's like $5,500 just in materials and the wall is 176 sq. ft. then another 52 linear feet for the caps.

What number per sq. ft. have you guys been hearing this year."

Doug said "I guess it depends on the type of wall system you are using and I am not familiar with the variety that you mentioned. We do some Keystone and Balcon walls that start at $45 per sq. ft. The best way to come up with a number is estimate it the way you have been. Make sure you are satisfied with the profit margin, and then convert that mathematically into a price per square foot."

Mike said "just to shed a little insight onto the wall pricing, there are several factors that determine the price. One very important factor is: Length of wall and height. A wall that is 1' tall and 400' long versus a 50 wall that is 6' tall. The 1st wall is 400 square face feet x ($35. per square face foot)=$14,000.00 the 2nd wall is 300 square face feet. x ($35. per square face foot)=$10,500.00

Which wall will be more profitable?

If you price these jobs by the square face and the price was the same for both, you would get KILLED on the 1st wall. I am sure that you already know that the hardest and most time consuming part of the wall construction is the foundation. For the most part, the foundation preparation should be the same (possibly a little more base material on the taller wall but this is not a big factor).

So if it takes 1 hour to dig out and prep 5' of foundation, and 1 hour of labor is priced at $55.00 per hour, about $550.00 in labor to prepare the 2nd wall and $4,400.00 to prepare the first wall. So this is why square footage pricing is dangerous. Please do not get me wrong, we do still price out our walls by the square face foot, however we do not have a fixed number. Also, the grade your are working with, finish grade, height of wall and grids needed, material selection, and project location are all very important factors that are not the same from job to job. I hope this helps."

Michael was asked, "What type of guarantees do you provide on your retaining wall builds? What would you suggest other lawn care business owners do?"

"As far as warranty, a one year in my opinion is standard however for some larger commercial projects that I have completed I have had to extend it to 2 year. In my opinion and through experience if the wall is going to move, it will do so within the first year anyway. Usually the first freeze and thaw are when most issues pop up. There are a lot of mechanics to building a wall that will determine the structure of the wall. If one has built a sound straight (meaning in line) wall and did not cut corners, there should be no worries about any warranty issues. I have had to fix some walls, and the honest reason is because we tried to cut corners that I thought were not important!

An example was that I was reading a set of plans and thought that the foundation be 18" thick and 1 course of wall should be buried. Well that would have been 26" down below grade from the top of dirt. Away we dug. Got to the site to check on the guys and do a foundation sign off and re-opened my plans to realize I made an 8" mistake. So I thought that I would try to save a few bucks and put 8" of disturbed soil back in and compact it with a grade-all (huge forklift type machine). The guys ran over that several times with the machine and then we set our foundation and laid the first block. As soon as we got a heavy rain, guess what happened... that dirt that we put back in settled. Guess who had to pay to repair it? Yup...trying to save $1,000 in gravel cost me about $20,000 in labor and replacing some material. GREAT lessen to learn!"

Once you are contacted by a potential client and meet with them to bid on their property, you aren't done yet. Remember to always follow up.

Kim asked "I was Just wondering after someone calls you for an estimate and you go out meet with them, and then submit a bid do most of them let you know if you didn't get the job or just kinda blow you off."

Tom answered "A few things will probably happen:

> 1. They will say something like "Geez, that is higher than I thought it would be." At this point you can either 1) haggle with the price or 2) tell them,"sorry, that is the price," and stick to your guns

> 2. They will say something like "when can you start. They

agree to the price and want you to do it."

3. Or they say "I will have to talk it over with my husband/wife." Nine times out of ten when someone says that, you probably will not get the bid. Now they will either call you back and tell you yes or no, or will not bother calling at all. I recommend that after a few days to give them a call up and ask them if they had any questions in regarding the bid. It helps get the ball rolling again."

Kim then asked "Okay how about commercial accounts, when they are excepting bids and say were not deciding until the middle of March. Should I call them back then or just hope to hear from them and if I didn't get it will they call and tell me. Or just let it go?"

Tom said "If you haven't heard anything after a while, then I would follow up with a phone call and even perhaps a letter."

Steve followed up by saying "I'm with Tom, follow up. Sometimes they want to see how interested you are and that just might make the deal for you."

How to bid on cemeteries.

One of our friends wrote us "I was thinking about bidding on a local cemetery here. It would be around a $88,000 year account. I think that in order to maintain the cemetery I am just going to hire on one guy and have him maintain the property on salary. There is a place for the equipment to be stored on site. I figure that it would give him around 40-50 hrs a week of work, a secure job, and I am able to probably make around a 50 to 60% profit margin on it. What do you think?"

Is this a good idea or a bad one and why so?

Joe said "Here are my thoughts. I think strictly from the business side of things this would be a good idea. It a good profit margin and would be relatively easy to job cost with just one guy on site each day. Having the equipment on-site is a bonus too... perhaps the worker would not even need a truck (although the cemetery is probably quite large so maybe a cart of some sort would be practical).

Here is how I see the cons to the idea:

- First of all I think it would be difficult to find the right guy to do this. I'm sure there are people out there who don't mind working alone each and every day but most would find this a huge disadvantage to the job (I know I would). As well since the person is working alone he would have to be experienced, motivated and very capable. Put these together and you have a rare person indeed. Not sure how large your company is but you could think about swapping the position around between your guys. This would break the monotony and allow fresh viewpoints on how the property is looking.

- On a similar note I have often said that the game of landscape maintenance is one best played with two. Not just for the human interaction but there are many jobs that just go smoother with 2 people. They can assist each other with difficult tasks and would be there for each other in the event of an emergency, which is not unheard of in our business.

- Customer's differ but I think that most customers think they are getting more value when they see multiple people on their site. If you did go with just the one guy I would send a whole crew in once in a while (say for major clean-ups) to bolster the perception of value in the customer's eyes and to make sure he feels important. Not sure if this is a factor for you with this contract.

There may be other pros and cons but these are the main ones from my point of view. Were it my contract I would probably consider sending 2 guys there for 2-3 days a week and sending them elsewhere on the remaining days."

How to get started offering holiday decoration and lighting services.

The winter months can be a tough time for a lawn care business. More and more lawn care businesses are getting into offering outdoor holiday lighting and decoration services to help them get through the slow times. Those who have experimented with it seem to be pretty happy with the results but how do you get started in offering these services?

Justin wrote "I'm just getting started in offering holiday decoration services and I'm really not sure how to go about bidding on hanging lights. I put a nice ad in my local newspaper and have been receiving responses. My going rate for lawn care is $60/hourly. Also the holiday lighting estimates will be for both putting up and taking the lights down. I will be using the customers lights. Should I possibly ask if I need to supply the product? I have a few customers already calling and I procrastinated. If someone could help me that would be awesome. Thanks."

Steve: "I would think since this is your first time doing this, why not decorate your house with some lights and figure out how long it takes you to do some standard lighting, such as running lights across the roof line. Figure out how long it takes by the linear foot. This should then help you measure other homes and get an idea how long the job will be.

Then if you are going to be taking them down as well, you will need to double that fee. Why not try and keep your hourly rate of $60 the same in your bids.

If you want to offer your own lights, why not consider figuring out how much lights are costing and buy them as needed. Charge the customer for the lights and then you will be able to take them down and reuse them next year as well. You could consider charging double the cost of the lights."

Charles: "I charge by the hour. I sell the clients the lights or they buy themselves. I put them up and take them down. When I take them down, I put them in some big Tupperware containers and put them in their garage. I know I could get a lot more because I've heard of guys doing a $1,000 a house and being very basic. I've been charging like $300 for a better job. It's still new to me though. I have looked at some of the "holiday lighting wholesellers" and they seem to be the same as a box store, so I just purchase them locally. If the client owns the lights then you explain that every year they will more than likely have to buy a few new sets because they go out. Plus if they want to expand on it they can do so a few pieces at a time.

It usually takes me until lunch for $150 and $150 to take them down which takes less time. You can make a lot more but once again I am new to this and am figuring out my costs."

Luke: "I installed 6 strings of 50 LEDS with a light clip for every light on a two story house. I charged by the hour and supplied the lights. It was a simple light around the roof job. The cost was $20 per box of lights and $5 dollars per box of 100 clips. It took 5.5 to 6 hrs to install. I charged $380.00."

Keep experimenting with offering holiday lighting and decoration services. Try to increase your sale price with each customer as you go. From the discussions I have had with other lawn care business owners who have done this for a few years, they try and shoot for $750 to $1,000 per house. This includes installing the decorations and taking them down. You can use your own decorations or use the customers. Try both ways and see which works best for you.

Getting started offering gutter cleaning services.

Offering gutter cleaning, at first can appear to be a daunting challenge, but don't let this stop you from making money on a service many others won't do. This is a great way to bring in extra income during the fall that can help your lawn care business when your mowing services slow down. One of our Gopher Lawn Care Business Forum members recently started his lawn care business and asked "this year is my first year in business and it has been a learning process for me. I need some help with something. In the fall other than racking leaves what else is there to do? I know a little about cleaning gutters but all I know to do is climb on a ladder and pull out the leaves. What else do I need to clean a gutter other than a ladder? Keep in mind that I'm on a low-budget. Also I live on the east coast and I don't know anything about charging for fall-clean ups so some tips on that would also be great."

John: "I have found that the best way to clean out gutters is with a blower....Back Pack preferred.

Charging for a leaf clean-up can be tough. Customers love to try and get the job done at a very cheap price. However, you have to think about several things when you do the estimate.

1. Are all the leaves off the trees?

2. How large is the property?

3. Do they want you to rid them or blow them into the

woods?

4. How long is it going to take to complete the work?

There are many options out there and leaf clean-up is a lot of work. So, charge by the hour for one and charge extra if they want you to take it away."

Keith: "Cleaning gutters is definitely big business for the Fall months. Cleaning gutters can be dangerous though so be sure to follow all safety regulations including fall protection.

Don't stop at simply cleaning the gutters though. **Offer a free inspection**.

- If you find loose fasteners you can replace them.
- If there is a leak at a joint, offer to repair it.
- You can also offer to install gutter leaf guards.

The list is endless. You can make tons of money between now and the end of the year if you price it right."

Howard: "Do you have a gas powered blower? Electric will work (if you have tons of cord) But the fastest way is to just get up on the roof and blow them out of the gutter. If you have a powerful gas blower be careful on the trigger as 283 mph wind from a gas blower will tear off the gutters. Then once you have the gutters cleaned out treat the job like any other kind of leaf removal service. If you don't have a blower i would suggest biting the bullet and buying a cheaper gas powered one. It will pay itself off in the fall very fast. I guarantee!"

Rich: "My experience has shown me that the fastest way to 'properly' clean out the gutters is to get up on a ladder and clean them by hand. I have used the blower attachments and they make a mess like no other. Especially if the gutters are wet. You'll find yourself cleaning off the roof, house, windows and yourself.

I charge $.50 per linear foot with a minimum charge of $45.00. Depending on your costs, overhead, dumping fees, etc...your price will differ depending."

I hope this discussion helps get you on the right track and gets you excited to offer this additional service in the fall. Remember each season presents you with great ways to make more money. You don't have to simply focus on cutting lawns.

How to charge for snow plowing.

With winter on it's way, many new lawn care business owners are looking to add snow plowing to their list of winter services. Trying to come up with an idea on how to charge can be challenging, especially for new businesses.

A Gopher Forum member asked such a question regarding snow plow services. "I have clients asking to have one payment for snow plowing their driveways for the winter season. Is there anywhere that one can get some sort of idea as to the expected snow for the season this year? I have searched everywhere, but found nothing. Realizing that predicting snowfall for any given year is about impossible, I am just wondering if anyone here has come up with an idea to supply this type of service. I did some last year, but lost each of them this year because we only had enough snow to plow 2 times, but they felt they paid a lot for just the 2 snow plows. I realize it is a gamble on both parties' side. I have real estate agents that are requesting a price for a seasons plow so it can be given as an incentive for a buyer, "Buy the house, get a years snow plowing and mow/trim." It is easy to calculate a years mow/trim. Any ideas would be greatly appreciated."

Pete: "I charge by the hour sometimes. My minimum for snow plowing small driveways is $35 under 6 inches of snow. Over 6 inches of snow I will charge 40% more. My hourly rate is $125/hr per truck. Salting or sanding the driveway or lot is 40% more. It is hard to price a job when you first get into snow removal. The actual removal is easy. If you have the right equipment you could make good money. I leave a invoice in their mailbox if they are not home, but I knock when I'm done with the job to see if they have cash or a check for me. If not then they have 10 days to send me the money or they will get charge a late fee."

Tim: "Here is how we charge for snow plowing:
$50 min for residential driveways every 2″ of snow fall. So if there is 6″ before we can get to them it would be $50 x 3 salt is $2.75 per pound spread.

We charge per push on commercial every 2″ of snow fall $3.00 per pound of salt spread.

For example. We have a commercial customer that has 4 miles of street and 4 mail stations.

We charge them $175 per push every 2″ of snow fall this includes 2 passes (1 down & 1 back) clearing cul-de-sac's and clearing mail stations, $3.00 per pound of salt used. Approx 1,000 lbs per application if we do all. We also stated in the contract we are not responsible to clear in front of or behind any cars/trucks street parked. Basically the contract states if the cars/truck get plowed in, we are not responsible to digging them out."

Ken: "Here's how we charge up here in the north east. The worst winter I've had is 9 storms, the best, 27. We average 12-15 winter storms. So here's what I offer:

- **Per push** - each time we come, we charge full time. I do my best to NOT allow any "inch-age" limits (i.e. 2″ then we come out, or push every two inches, etc.) because truthfully, everyone has a different idea of what 2″ is and it's just one more place for conflict. If I have a commercial account and they INSIST on that verbiage, I accept and hope for the best, but I would NOT accept any "cut in pay" if I missed the 2″ mark. We charge full price each push, $15 minimum - most of mine are $20-$25 per push. I charge $5-$10 to cleanup the end of the driveway if needed after the storm.

- (**NOTE:** I do not offer "per storm". If someone insisted on it, I'd just charge 2-2.5 times my per push rate and hope for the best)
- **Per season** - with insurance. I don't offer a blanket "per season" charge because there is WAY too much variance in the amount of snow we get. It would be like saying "I'll build you a house for $125,000 and then hoping you decide on a 900 sf ranch and not a 2,000 sf colonial. What I do is figure 15 storms, 2 visits per storm. Let's say it's $25 per push, their contract would be $25 x 2 x 15 or $750. This amount would cover them from a minimum of 11 storms to a maximum of 18 storms. If we had less than 11, they'd get some refund, if more than 18, they'd get a bill. THIS gives them a 90% probability, give or take, of meeting their "budgeted" amount, but also covers us from extremes.

A final word, ALL my plowing is per push, every single one. BUT I think it's nice to have a variety. You get more from the contracts during times of little snow, but you get some big money from the "per push" people during heavy winters. It's sort of like diversifying your stock portfolio."

Should you raise or lower your lawn care prices in winter?

When winter comes, the lawn care and landscaping industry jobs tend to slow down. Which leads me to this great question that was asked on the Gopher Forum. "It's winter time and work is becoming scarce. So when a customer calls me and I go out to give them a bid I've been sticking to my regular prices for cleanups or whatever it might be.

Does anyone raise prices because it's winter because of less work around?

Lower prices because it's winter to make sure they get the job?

Or just stay the same.

I been staying at my prices but not to many are accepting my bids. I can't really be too picky with jobs now so I try to keep it a little on the conservative side.
When I was busy it didn't really matter if they didn't accept because I had a month long waiting list.

What are your thoughts on this?"

Tom: "Here is my 2 cents worth on it.

   1). I NEVER change pricing from season to season as a general rule.

   (Why? because customers talk. If you have customer 1 that you did in November and now a customer 2 in December for the same job like leaf clean up and your rate for the customer 1 was say $45 an hour and now customer 2 is now $65 this may cause conflicts, because customer 1 may have referred customer 2. We don't always remember to ask "How they heard about us?" but we should make it a habit to ask, and most of the time new customer don't offer to tell us that they were referred by a previous customer.) Does that make sense?

NOTE: I know every job is different. One may have more leaves than another or want some extra work done but when comparing apples to apples, keep the pricing close.

2). Now this also depends on the status of you and your families well being, if you haven't worked very much and bills are piling up then by all means raise or lower your rates as you see fit. When I first stated my contractors business I went through hard times as do most new business men and women. So this is called "FEAST or FAMINE" and we all go through these times it is the nature of the beast.

3). The Holiday season is here and almost over so things are going to be tight for everyone for a few months. So to get more jobs you can offer lower rate for the Holidays as a selling point and this will excuse rule #1 and bring you to rule #2. Basically only you know what would be acceptable for doing a certain job, this is all about how much is your time worth? If a job is presented to you and you have a bill to pay and you only charge enough to pay that bill then fine do it, as long as it keeps your head above water.

4). It is hard to do this sometimes but everyone in business especially this industry needs to save for "Rainy Days". With the majority of this industry being seasonal "Feast and Famine" always comes and sits on us for a longer period of time than with other businesses. My grand-father told me this and I didn't learn what "RAINY DAYS" were until I was like 30 something. I always had jobs and money so I didn't save and found myself in hard times scratching and scraping for work. Just bare with it and hang on tight maybe try some new services to offer to generate some work that may not have been there. Fortunately for me, my wife works seasonal at the IRS and it runs parallel with our lawn care and landscaping season, so we bank her money to live on through the off season months.

I want to also mention, this is good general business advice for everyone. Most of us have gone through this situation or are going through this so the boat is getting full. I commend you for bring this topic to light.

One idea we use is a Christmas fund at the bank. Start one and put money in it to cover seasonal living expenses. These accounts draw little to no interest but the money is there in late October for you to move into another account to live from. It works only if you stick to putting the amounts in it each month you set up. If your short one month and can make it up the next then do it, don't spend the extra money on something else, you have to be disciplined in this. If you want to continue to be in the lawn care or landscaping business and survive the "Feast and Famine" or "Rainy Days", you need to do this."

How your lawn care business can winterize irrigation systems and make money.

Winterizing lawn irrigation systems is a great add on service that is easy to do and can bring you in some good money in the fall. John wrote in to the Gopher Forum and asked how to do this.

John: "Hi guys I have a question. Do you think a 25 CFM @ 175 PSI, 13 HP horizontal air compressor would be ok to use to blow out residential homes? I got a contract with a realty company with 50 properties. The previous lawn care company did not blow out the systems last year. I have been fixing all of the lawn care customers irrigation systems and mowing their lawns."

Junior: "It should work. I would never use a tow behind though. Remember, DO NOT blow air for more than 2 minutes through the zone. Air compress more than water, and it heats up BIG TIME! You will melt the irrigation pipe if you go crazy with the air."

Rob: "I agree with Junior. Make sure you use it no more than 2 minutes and no higher than 40 psi or you run the risk of damaging the vacuum pressure valve and the solenoid zone valve. Also you will need to have a compressor that will deliver a min 5 cfm @ 40 psi."

Steve: "Do you have any suggestions on when to market this service?"

Rob: "Marketing for sprinkler winterization should be started in the Aug - Sept time frame. You can also get on the phone and talk to your current costumers about your winterization. You might consider offering a discount for being a mowing client. Also do not forget about those estimates you did during the mowing season that you did not land. Those lawn care estimates are still potential customers for other services. Ask your current clients to spread the word and if a potential customer says no, try to get the last word in i.e. "well if you know of some one that needs our service please give them my information.""

Second make sure you are ready to go. Check your equipment out good. You can't afford to have a compressor go down, especially if you have 6-7 blow-out for the day. It pays to have a backup compressor."

Luke: "I just finished winterizing the irrigation systems of all my customers. I used a large tow behind diesel compressor. The air line was a 1 inch diameter hose. The air hoses came in 50 ft lengths. The average yard needed two lengths to reach to the blow out bib. The compressor had a gate valve for air control. The bib adapter also had a gate valve. The 100 ft of hose didn't heat up at all.

Costs:

- The compressor rental ended up costing $100 for the compressor for the day.
- $10.00ea for the 50 ft hoses.
- So for $120.00 I rented out a compressor.
- I used about $20.00 in diesel to top off the tank.

It took me about an hour at each job site. So doing 6-7 places in a day and paying approx $140.00 for the rental.

You can do the math. I charged each lawn care customer $60.00 - $70.00 per blow out.

Profit:

- (7 customers) x ($70 per customer) = $490
- ($490 gross income) - ($140 expenses) = $350 profit per day."

Why the cheapest lawn care bid doesn't always win.

New lawn care business owners tend to enter the market by bidding their jobs lower than others. This may work at times but as you grow, you will see problems with this lawn care marketing attack plan. The first problem is that you may be losing money on the work you are doing or just barely breaking even. The second problem is that you are most likely attracting cheap lawn care customers who only want cheap service. Cheap customers tend to not want any upsells and they are usually your biggest complainers.

As you try to apply this concept to commercial property maintenance there is a tendency to exacerbate the problem. Larger properties will bring larger estimate amounts. However, you may find yourself so fixated on the dollar value of the bid that you fail to calculate your actual costs. You may also find yourself buying larger commercial equipment and then having to hire a staff. This has brought on the ruin of many a lawn care business.

Some commercial property managers know this is a problem and they hate signing up a lawn care maintenance company at the beginning of the year only to have them go out of business half way through the year. They also won't go simply with the lowest bid, because they want quality work.

Marcus wrote us on the Gopher Forum "I'm new at this so I didn't think it would be this hard to get my lawn care business started. I get lots of calls for estimates but I never get any."

Keith: "It's good that you are getting lots of calls. Your advertising must be working.

What are your customer's reactions when you give estimates? Is your price too high or do they say they will think about it and just never call you back?

There are many steps in professional and effective lawn care estimating.
I will list two ideas.

> 1) Sell quality. Don't let potential customers pick someone else simply because your bid is a few dollars higher. Let them know that you do quality work and that you are dependable. Take your potential customers for tours of their lawns as you give estimates. Point out areas that you will pay attention too and show them how you can make a dramatic improvement in their yard.

> 2) Be ready to work immediately. I have found when doing estimates if I have my equipment with me and I can work immediately they often say "go ahead" right away. Once they see a quality job they almost always sign on as regular customers.

Knowing and following all the steps will greatly increase your acceptance ratio."

Steve: "What kinds of jobs are you getting called for?"

Marcus: "The jobs are luxury condos the normal price is $80 to $85 dollars a month on each unit. I bid $70 a month.

The condo property maintenance is handled by a condo

association and they range from 24 units to 36 units. The way I found out it was $80 to $85 a unit is by asking some guys that have been maintaining the property for years. They condo association has told me they received cheaper estimates but then they said (we go for the best service not the best price.) That's what they say and then end up not giving me work."

So remember, start small, scale up step by step. Build profits and gain an understanding of what you need to charge to make a profit. Only make the jump to commercial properties once you have a firm understanding of how to run your business based on servicing residential properties.

Don't try to compete with $15 bucks a cut, stand out and command a premium.

Are you finding yourself trying to compete with fly by night lawn care businesses that advertise they will cut a lawn for $15? Don't try to compete with them. Any customer who hires such a lawn care business will quickly find out how unreliable they are. You don't want these cheap customers anyway because they will be the ones most likely to complain. Instead why not follow the steps these other lawn care business owners have taken. Be personable. Meet with your new potential clients. Offer them an incentive to prepay for their lawn care and give them the best service you can.

Charles: "I've found because there is so much competition in my area that lawn care prices are held down a bit. Once you have a good lawn care customer base & you give them good service you can:

- Raise prices a bit more as you've had a chance to prove yourself to them
- Go higher on new estimates as you don't really "need" every new customer.

Now I am, to the best of my knowledge, competitively priced for my area as far as my per cut prices. Some are higher & I think that is attributed to being well established as I stated above. But there are advertisements in the newspaper here and on the internet for my area that promote $15 bucks a lawn mowing! Granted most of them are probably in it for extra beer money & are unreliable to their customers but my potential customers see those advertisements too & know if I bid $35 per lawn mowing they can get it for probably half that however lousy the service may be.

My annual/monthly clients are required to pay by the 1st of each month for the following months service. I'm afraid of cutting for a month billing them net 30 then cutting for another month & finding 2 months in that they don't pay so that's the only way I will bill for that type of customer.

Do you offer incentive for your clients to sign an annual instead of staying per cut? How do you pull that off?"

Shane: "Sure I offer incentives. It has helped me find better lawn care customers as well. I no longer will mow someone's lawn on a "per cut" basis. I have found out that those type of customers are not the ones we should be looking for.

You always "need" new lawn care customers. This is how you grow your business unless you are comfortable with keeping it a one man show. I personally don't want to stay in the labor end of the business forever.

I have the same advertisements here too but we must not try to run our business the way everyone else runs theirs. Get a business plan and stick to it. That's what I did and it's proving to be successful so far. Also, the people that a "$15.00 a cut" ad attracts are NOT the customers you want. I had to learn that the hard way."

Chad: "I think I am in the same boat as both of you. I am trying to find a good overall price to charge my lawn care customers. This is my first year really trying to push the lawn care. The lawns I work on are a lot bigger than what most people mention here. The houses all sit on 1/2 acre lots if not bigger. The houses average 2,200-2,400 sq ft, 2 car garages with long driveways. When I started calculating everything my game plan is to charge $35-$40 a cut, **offering a 15% discount for the customers who**

sign a year contract and pay up front.

Now I thought I was reasonable priced until my clients start getting quotes for $20-$23 a cut. Luckily I have 6 yrs of sales & marketing behind me. By presenting my lawn care flyers that are professionally laid out and knocking on every door I hung a flyer on, I was able to sway every customer to spend the $15-20 extra. I personally couldn't believe it and neither could my girl friend who helped me distribute the flyers. The only problem with this strategy is that I don't cover much ground. Out of 100 houses, I talked to maybe 1 to 3 people who were receptive and willing to sign a lawn care contract.

The way you present yourself is everything. You're not selling a product, you are selling a service. I am always more expensive. I don't try to be. I just don't want to work enough to just pay my bills and break even. I hope this helps."

What's more profitable for a lawn care business, small or large yards?

What's more profitable for a lawn care business, small or large yards? This is such a great question and I am glad it was brought up on the Gopher Forum. There are up sides and down sides to going each way. For instance, if you service a lot of smaller accounts, no one customer will be monopolizing your time and if they cancel, it won't be a big shock to your business. However you will need to travel in between these jobs which will increase your wind shield time or drive time. As we have learned, you aren't making money when you are driving so you want to minimize the amount of time spent driving between lawn care customers.

Having a larger property to maintain can be beneficial because you will be providing lawn care on a larger area without having to drive around too much. Something to watch out for especially when you are bidding on larger properties is that new lawn care business owners have a tendency to underbid jobs. They just see $$$$ signs and aren't taking into consideration how much it will actually cost them to service such a yard. This can lead to breaking even on large jobs or even losing money on them if you aren't careful. Let's learn more on this topic by talking to Shawn about how he prices lawn care for his business.

Shawn: "Prices vary depending on the market. No matter what, I suggest that you set a minimum charge for lawn care. My minimum charge is $35 with prices going up from there. This is for mowing, trimming, edging, and blowing off the grass clippings. However, I was talking to a guy from Florida on here last week who said that he couldn't get more than $25 a mow in his area. He even mows some lawns for as low as $15. What I'm saying is you must find out what your competition is charging, and what the market supports. Also, you must make money on each account. If you are not you must be charging more. Once you get going, figure out what your cost per yard is, and then set a minimum PROFITABLE price based on that assessment."

Steve: "How do you estimate lawn service? Do you charge per acre or how do you charge?"

Shawn: "I do not charge by the acre. You should have a hourly rate for which you want your company (not yourself to earn). Mine is $45 per man hour. For example, If you have a large property that takes two guys one hour to mow you should be charging at least $90. It is ok to let this rate vary down a little bit, but not a lot. Like I said, my minimum charge is $35 which would be for a smaller, regular size yard in a residential neighborhood. I have one property that is about 5 acres(approx). It takes 2 guys about 3.5 hours to mow, trim, edge, and blow off. I charge them $250 per mowing.

Also, if you are doing fall cleanups. Make sure you are getting at least $45 per man hour on those."

Steve: "What kind of equipment are you using on the larger properties and how do you estimate fall leaf cleanups?"

Shawn: "This one large property I service is owned by a demanding customer who has extra high expectations. When I say it is 5 acres, this is 5 acres of well manicured fescue that the customer wants bagged. I actually only use a ride on mower with a 48″ cut for most of the mowing. He has an area up around the house that he likes to be push mowed. This is done with a 21″ push mower. I run Stihl FS 100 RX 4 mix trimmers, and edger. He has a driveway that is approximately 200 yards long that is flanked by pine trees.

Consequently, when trimming around the pine trees, the driveway becomes littered with pine cones. A large backpack blower is required to clear them in a timely manner. This is one of the accounts I inherited from my previous employer. When I was there we usually had 3 guys on it with 2 ride on mowers. This knocked the time down to 2-2.5 hours. Usually closer to 2.5 hours.

I think fall cleanups are tough to bid. I usually try to help my regular customers out, and just charge them a leaf removal charge, depending on how much longer it takes us to mow it. I break down my per man hour charge into minutes. For instance $45 per man hour equals .75 cents a minute. If it takes two guys 10 minutes longer than it does to mow I would charge them $15 dollars extra. $1.50 per min x 10 minutes.

For non customers, who only receive one cleanup at the end of the season…a good rule of thumb is to charge twice the amount that you would charge to mow. However if the property has a high amount of leaves and complications such as beds that are tough to get to, or water features you should charge more."

Steve: "What has been you experience on servicing high end properties and large properties. Would you prefer most of your lawns to be large like this and high end?

Or would you prefer your ideal lawns to be smaller and not so high end?"

Shawn: "I would prefer for all of my accounts to be high end. It helps company morale a lot if you are taking care of high end accounts. I have found that employees take a greater sense of pride in their work when servicing high end accounts. As far as the size goes, both large and small have their positives. The thing I like about large, high-end properties I just mentioned is that you are there for an extensive amount of time and always producing.

The truck stays put, and you are getting output for the whole time. You can make the same amount of money mowing 5 or 6 smaller yards in the same amount of time, but your rig has to move from account to account. Therefore, I think the larger accounts are more cost effective. The downside to the larger accounts is that it tends to tire you and your employees faster, rather than getting a break from yard to yard."

How to price and trim hedges.

Trimming hedges quickly and easily can be tough along with coming up with the right price for your lawn care bid. Let's look at this discussion from the Gopher Forum on how to price and trim hedges.

Sherman: "I hate doing hedges, but I seem to get a lot of customers wanting me to do them. I am good at the hedges themselves, no problems there, what makes me hate them so much is this. When a client has mulched under all there hedges, how the hell do you get all the darn leaves out of the mulch after trimming the hedges??? There has to be a better way then getting on your knees for an hour or more picking the dam things out by hand. I tried using the blower on low, high just makes a big mess . Any insight would be very much appreciated."

Brandon: "Here's what I do. I have 2 large tarps, I lay them down and scoot them up under the hedges. The tarps are 16 ft. long. Then when I'm done cutting, I just fold up the corners and drag all the clippings away. It is a 1 minute clean-up. Much easier than raking everything out of the way first."

Shane: "How often do you trim the hedges? I generally trim hedges once or twice a year, and mulch at the same time."

Chad: "I would say it depends. Is this included in your monthly agreement? Or do you charge extra?

For me… Mine are all on monthly contracts and hedges are included. So to keep the mess to a minimum, I may trim them twice a month.

The tarp thing… Well It is a good idea I see home owners do it that way, but no lawn care business owners doing it that way. Most just take the blower and either blow the clipping to the lawn then mulch it all up, that's what I do. Or just blow them around under the hedges which will help mix them up in the mulch.

Maybe go buy a cheap gas powered leaf blower with the ability to convert to a leaf sucker upper. I have a small gas blower that does that and have used it to suck up clippings. But in mulch it will suck up some of the mulch as well..

Florida is different than any other state. If we only trimmed hedges twice a year, We'd have to trim feet off instead of a few inches. Trimming hedges is a monthly thing down here.. ALL YEAR…"

Dave: "Also, if you don't have one, get a pole hedge trimmer, as long as the hedge is under 10′ or so, you don't need a ladder at all. With the tilting head, you can trim the top of the hedge much easier too."

Greg: "Whenever somebody asks me to trim their shrubs I never know if I'm overpricing or giving them a sweet deal I would never give."

Chad: "What is your hourly labor rate? Look at them and see how long it will take you. If you charge $50 per hour on labor and you think it will take you 30 minutes to trim the shrubs. Then quote them at $25.

If your new to bidding, take your time. You will under/over bid until you get the hang of it. Also don't rush your bid and make bigger mistakes by guessing way to high or way too low."

Tim: "I would say $65 hr for hedge trim."

How to estimate and market stump grinding.

I had a great opportunity to interview Erin who offers stump grinding services and sells used stump grinders about the business of stump grinding.

Steve: "Can you share with us some of your insight on how a lawn care business owner can best make money with stump grinders?

How much could they make using such stump grinders?"

Erin: "The first thing you do is put your phone number on the grinder. Especially on the back of the grinder. Get business cards printed with space for a cost estimate you can write in. Going rate in my area is $5 per inch of stump with a $100-150 minimum. Measure across the widest part of the stump.

Don't haggle over an inch or two, just write the estimate. With these grinders a 36″ stump might take 20 minutes, you figure your hourly rate from there.

As you go about your daily lawn care service routine, keep a sharp eye out for stumps. Knock on doors and leave a card with the estimate, or note the address and mail one with pricing. Contact your local tree services. Even if they have their own grinder, tell them to call if they get too busy or it's broke down.

Take out a small classified ad for a month or two, introducing your service. Hand out cards to your existing customers or mail with their bill. Look for dead trees, they have a habit of leaving a stump later. On the weekend go for a drive with your grinder and listen out for chainsaws. The only reason a chainsaw makes noise is cuttin' trees. Pull up and introduce yourself. There's lots of ways to get work for the machine.

Golf courses can't have stumps because the mower operators always hit them. It costs more to fix the mower once than grinding the stump to eliminate the problem forever.

Remember that clean-up and hauling away the debris is EXTRA charge. That's where one of our pick-up dump kits comes in very handy. Dig a big enough stump hole and you can charge to bring them back topsoil to fill it."

Jim: "Here is another way to estimate stump grinding jobs. Stump Grinding (Chip) Per Inch of Stump Diameter $ 3.00 /inch."

Create a check list to win over commercial lawn care jobs.

Here are a few great ideas on how to land commercial lawn care jobs. Consider creating a check list to win over commercial jobs.

John: "I need some help here. The new lawn care season will be coming and I was wondering how lawn care business owners find out which lawn care contracts are up for bids for commercial areas as well as housing addition common areas, etc? I have looked at public notices in the newspaper and emailed property management companies with little to no luck. What do I need to do?? Thanks"

Ken: "Emailing is a good first step but don't stop there. You have to get your name in front of them and in their heads.

Pick up the phone to find out who you need to speak to. Get the name of the purchasing manager.

Pound the pavement to pay them visits. On your first visit, bring flyers, business cards, and photos of previous (current) lawn care projects.

On your second visit, bring your lawn care equipment. Invite the purchasing manager outside to see that you have the equipment necessary to complete their lawn work in a timely manner and with professional results.

Never take the first three "NOs" as a defeat."

Chris: "I never take my trailer to a commercial lawn care estimate. I think you look smaller when you show up by yourself with a bunch of stuff. I did this once and was asked if I thought I could do it alone. I told them that due to rain I gave my guys the day off. I didn't get the lawn care work. I like to go to the site an hour ahead of our meeting so I can walk the whole place. I make a list of what I see and make it a point to tell them that I would never allow this to happen. I came up with a list of 25 reasons for a property management company to switch to us. This is just a list of the most common problems I've seen in my time. This gives them something to judge their current contractor by. A lot of them don't even know the place has a problem. I just put in a bid for a local commercial facility's lawn and I was standing in the entrance for about 20 min. waiting for the head maintenance man. When he got there I had a list of 22 lawn care problems that I would fire my father for. Now he knows that we know what he needs without him saying a word."

How your lawn care business should price a fall leaf cleanup.

Leaf raking can be a very profitable job for a lawn care business. But you must be aware of some common traps in raking a customer's lawn.

Leaf raking is a big profit point in the lawn care industry. Damp leaves left clumped on a lawn can damage grass. They clog gutters and down spouts. They also make flower and shrub beds look untidy.

A Gopher Forum member shared with us this leaf clean up story. "A new customer called to get an estimate for raking the yard and cleaning out gutters. He had several large trees in his yard. Although his yard was covered with leaves more than half of the leaves were still on his trees. Since he had a mulching area to keep me from having to haul off his leaves, I gave an estimate of $150. He did not want to spend that much and said that if I would do it for $110, he would let me cut his yard next summer. The leaf job went well and I collected my money and went home. The next day he called to say that I had not raked all the leaves and that I needed to come back by. I explained that the leaves in his yard had fallen after I had finished and that I was not responsible for those leaves. Not wanting to lose his business next year, I went back and did a quick touch up job which took an hour. Still, I was satisfied as it was a big yard and I would get to do his mowing work all the following year.

When Spring rolled around, I took my equipment to his house and was told that someone else had already been contracted to mow the lawn for the season. I reminded him of our agreement and he said that the other people were doing it for $5 less than my estimate.

Though it made me mad, I didn't think too much about it until the next fall when he called and said that his other lawn care company had quit and he wanted me to rake his leaves again. My response was to remind him of our previous agreement and I told him the price for leaves alone would be $250. He declined saying he would get someone else to do it.

I learned a few lessons from this customer.

1. I did not have a signed agreement - You should be very careful about taking a customer's word that they will let you do their lawn "next season" in return for a cheaper price today. If the agreement is verbal it is very easy for a customer to back out of the agreement.
2. Price each job as an individual effort - If a leaf job is worth $250 to you then bid it accordingly. Do not let the potential of other work influence your price significantly downward. That other work may never materialize.
3. Explain to the customer that leaves on the trees are not included in the price - Leaves continue to fall through the entire season. If you contract to do a leaf job, let the customer know that any leaf droppage that occurs after the job is done is not covered under the quoted price.

Leaf pickup is very easy to under price. A job which looks like it should take less than 1 hour can often wind up taking 4 times that long. Take extra caution when giving estimates."

Tom said "Your leaving money on the table if you are offering leaf and gutter cleanup by the hour.

If you are called to a residential property just for gutter clean out you should be charging by the foot and it should include down spout flushing. $1 a ft and if its 2 story it should be a little extra

for the height. *ALWAYS PRACTICE SAFETY WHEN WORKING OFF LADDERS AND ON ROOFS, AND INJURY CAN TAKE YOU OUT OF THE GAME COMPLETELY, COSTING YOU MORE THAN MONEY.*
If your doing a fall clean up,(leaf clean up and removal) gutter clean out should be included. Plant beds are not extra either, they are a part of the lawn.

These are common practices within my area."

Steve: "Very interesting! So when you give a bid for a fall yard cleanup, do you include a line item that shows gutter cleaning and a price for that? Do you include another line item for plant beds? Or are all these included into one price and it isn't broken down at all?"

Tom: "We here by propose to; clear all lawn and plant bed ares of leaves to the best of our ability. Clean and flush all gutters and down spouts as follows,

Fall Lawn Clean Up $$$$$$
(All lawn and plant bed areas)

Gutter Clean Out $$$$$$
(Cleaning and flushing all gutter & down spouts)

Total Due $$$$$$

If the customer balks at the gutter charges then explain to them the importance of having them cleaned out. Most will go for it."

Offer a home safety inspection as part of your lawn care estimate procedure.

Here is a novel idea. What if you offered a home owner property safety inspection along with your free lawn care estimate?

Consider these old axioms: "People buy from people they like." and "Fear motivates most purchasing."

You could walk the property with the home owner and explain how certain bushes need to be trimmed or maybe re-landscaped. How you would suggest new landscape lighting for the nighttime. I bet an entire upsell package could be create!

Pete: "Great idea. I used to do that as part of my community policing efforts. Time to make some money with it!

Some ideas for a check list regarding safety and crime prevention inspections.

Windows:

Never allow any bushes, trees, flowers, etc., to grow enough to block the view of a window. Good rule of thumb is this, if you are inside and can't clearly see what is outside, the window is obscured.

Trees should not be allowed to grow next to a house. Trees can be climbed to wherever a window or ledge is. They can also fall into the house with enough wind pushing them.

If ornamental growth is something the homeowner wants, steer them towards bushes and such that have lots of thorns and similar barbs and sharp edges. Should a crook cut himself on thorns, blood and tissue samples, if found, can be analyzed for DNA. DNA science has evolved to a point where almost anything touched can be examined for evidence. More and more states have DNA data banks making it easier to get a match.

Don't make it easy to get in. Keep the windows upstairs and down, locked. Secure and reinforce if needed, air conditioners with screws and other means to keep them from being pushed or pulled out. I had a case where the burglar hung onto the edge of the roof with one hand and managed to get inside after forcing the window open.

Doors:

Keep the growth in check like you would for windows. More than one mugging has occurred when somebody jumped out from behind the bushes to ambush the arriving homeowner. The element of surprise works against you.

Do not keep any keys hidden nearby like under the door mat or hanging on one of the bushes. Find another location away from any structures.

Deadbolts.

Make sure they reach well into the door frame. Better still, make sure that area is reinforced to resist breaking the frame and door. Metal devices that fit over the door and held in place by the deadbolt covers are good for this. Don't be afraid to use more than one deadbolt. The force to break down the door will have to be spread over a larger area requiring far more effort to get in. Time is your friend in this case.

Lighting:

Motion detector lights are highly recommended. You can now get them so that additional lights come on inside the house after the outside lights are tripped on. Just be sure and adjust them correctly. It's been my experience that it will take a few tries to get it just right.

Motion detection lights should be aimed wherever areas of the property that are not well seen can be illuminated and/or allowing the occupant to see who or what is outside ringing the door bell or whatever.

Should a street light style light be preferred by a homeowner, beware there is a formula for determining the correct height vs. lumens (brightness). Can't get my hands on it just yet, the idea is not to light up the place like Area 51. You have neighbors to contend with and possibly local ordinances addressing it. They also cost a bunch more to purchase, mount, and operate.

Stuff lying around:

Never leave ladders outside where they can be "borrowed" to gain access to your house. Keep them inside if possible or secured with good quality chain or cable with locks.

Keep wooden fences in good condition and replace any weak or broken pieces. They are handy for breaking windows and for use as a battering ram.

Secure hand tools like shovels, rakes, anything with a handle, for the same reason as above.

Alarms systems:

If somebody is bound and determined to get inside, nothing short of Fort Knox will keep them out. Remember that if the house is secure enough to keep somebody from breaking in, you will have a difficult time getting out in an emergency situation. This is something to strongly consider if the occupant is not healthy. I've seen it when chainsaws were needed to get inside to rescue a person in critical need of health care.

A good alternative is an alarm system. It doesn't keep anybody out, it just lets you as well as somebody else know that something is wrong.

Fire, burglary, panic, and medical emergencies can all be addressed with today's systems.

Having said that, there is a golden opportunity for the sales rep to sell a bill of goods that is more than what's required.

KISS. Keep It Simple Stupid.

Door sensors:

Some area coverage via infrared sensors and a choice of silent or noisy enunciation is all you really need. Optional would be daytime vs. night time operation. That type of operation activates certain sensors while you are in the house or away from it. Forget all the wizbang stuff. "

What freebies work to get lawn care contracts signed?

When you are trying to get a new potential lawn care client to sign up with an annual lawn care contract, sometimes you may want to offer some kind of inducement to get them to jump on it. Maybe some of these ideas will help you craft your own lawn care contract promotion.

Matt: "What are some good specials to offer new clients to sign up for an annual lawn care contract? Like one month free with signed contract? I know different people react to different offers. Let's say I did offer the one month of free free lawn care, for EXAMPLE: Jan - cut one week free, Feb - cut one week free, Mar - cut one week free, Apr - cut one week free..... That would equal a month of free of lawn care service but it would be divided up into those months. Do you think that would work?"

Chuck: "I would make it the last month free. It's the only way to be sure you get the other 11 paid in full. If you give it to them quickly and they split after 6 months then you are out!

Matt: "Yeah I have noticed, when you do a verbal agreement for 12 months and shake hands, you tend to get burned in the winter season. Ultimately the goal of the contract is that you are making money in the winter months.

We lawn care operates have to make a living also, we have bills, we have a family to feed, mortgages and all just like anyone else.

I guess they don't care or understand. They still have there job in the winter."

Chestin: "As far as what to offer for yearly contracts, to be honest, the only way to find out what works is to test different offers. A free month's lawn care service is a great thing to test, but you never know how it might compare to something like a free core aeration and overseeding in the fall. Or a free gutter cleaning. Or maybe even a restaurant gift certificate.

Again, you never know what will work best until you test a couple of different options."

The benefits of and how to sell annual lawn care contracts.

Having your lawn care customers on annual contracts can be very beneficial especially during the winter months. If you are not so good budgeting out your money and tend to spend what you have, then maybe having lawn care customers pay you an equal amount each month would be the way to go. The customer can benefit from this as well because they will be paying the same price every month and they can easily fit it into their budget.

What is the best way to present the annual lawn care contract concept to your customers?

Charles: "People are hesitant to to sign up & pay $70-100 per month to you when they just met you & the next few months the grass doesn't grow much.

I seem to have better luck during the summer with simply saying verbally: I also offer monthly billing, I know Mrs. Smith that $30 a week is a lot to pay for lawn care & this time of year that can mean $120 -$150 a month! So here's what I do, I'll do it for $100/ month year round. It's more budgetable for you & I can better budget my business knowing exactly what's coming in. Basically, I agree to make less during the Summer & Fall & you agree to help me feed the wife & kids in the winter time. Either way it's up to you ma'am. Which way would you prefer?

With this concept, I did pretty well, No I didn't get every one to sign up but I'd say more than half to choose the contract option!

The property lots here in our area are 80'x125' and if they are on a corner they're a little bigger. Last summer provided it's a normal house (normal amount of landscaping, fences, ditches to line trim around) I would quote $25/cut or $85/mo year round. I didn't specify much as far as frequency other than to say during growing season I'd be there weekly & out of season It's usually about twice a month. On a corner lot it was usually $30/cut or $100/mo.

A couple months ago as things slowed down with the per cut customers I really learned the value of those annual accounts & I need to stack on more annual accounts over the summer to be in better shape next winter. So I found a way to get the pricing more competitive & lean the cards so I would get more annual accounts than per cut (in theory anyway we'll see). Part of my new proposal form looks like this:

> This proposal is for: the property at the address above. Normal services include mowing, line trim, edging, blow off all concrete walkways/driveways.
>
> In this proposal the monthly fees are based on 34 services (visits) per calendar year as follows:
> Month = # of visits to be made under this agreement :
> Jan.= 1, Feb.= 1, Mar.= 2, *Apr.= 2, May= 3, June= 4, July= 4, Aug.= 5, Sept.= 5, Oct.= 3, Nov.=2, Dec.=2
>
> Billing options: *Per cut (weekly In summer months) $ * * wk or Monthly billing with annual agreement $ * * per month.
> So for example the same lawn I had been quoting $25/cut or $85 /mo. before I would now do this.
>
> If I want $25/ cut: *$25 x 34 services/yr = $850 divided by 12 months is $70.83. Rounded up I quote $25/cut ot $71/month.
>
> My prices are more competitive & I still make $25/cut

when all is said & done.

If they need an extra cut in there its just that… extra!"

Now that is a very interesting way to sell the concept of the annual lawn care contract to new lawn care customers. Consider this when you are out there signing up lawn care customers as well. You might find the monthly price you quote on an annual contract, a little easier for the home owner to accept. You still get paid the same amount in the long run but the monthly prices are cheaper for the customer.

The danger of large lawn care accounts.

It seems like every year I hear a similar story in different variations. A new business is just getting itself stabilized with a hand full of customers when a large account seems to be calling them from up high atop a mountain of promised money. The call becomes so enticing that the entrepreneur can not stop themselves from holding back.

Does the beginning of this story sound familiar?

This time the story revolves around a lawn care and fence installation business. The business had been started the previous year with just the owner running it with a helper from time to time. The owner also had a full time job to cover his expenses. All was going fine. The business was growing slowly until that fateful phone call came in. This large commercial property needed lawn care and a fence installed.

The job was going to be a big job but the owner was going to have to float the project for 60-90 days. That is how long it would take to get his first payment. Could the owner do it the caller asked. A big fat five figure project was just waiting for him if he said yes. So he gambled and said what the heck, I deserve this, this is my time to step up, and he said yes.

At the time he started this job, he had managed to save a few thousand dollars. He thought this would be enough to get him and a few helpers through the next 2 month or so. The next day, he quit his full time job and showed up to this commercial facility to start work.

The grass was tall and unkept so it took more time than normal to cut it down. The fencing. Where do I begin. The fencing was going to cost him big money that he didn't have. He would have to pay for this on his credit card. He would also have to buy a large commercial mower on his credit card. But there was no risk right? I mean he would most certainly make his money back on all this and them some. Right?

Within a handful of days from the time he took the call. He had quit his steady full time job. He had hired a few extra helpers. He had depleted his savings and gone into a 5 figure credit card debt.

After the first month he submitted his invoice and he was elated. Never had he submitted such a big invoice to anyone in the past. He was finally a big lawn care business. He already had plans to upgrade his truck and trailer. He made it.

The second month rolled on and he started to get nervous, especially when he saw the for sale sign go up. He called and asked about that. Surely he was still going to get paid right? Oh sure they said, you will be paid. He was getting worried because he figured he had about 3 more weeks of living on his credit card before it was maxed out.

Now do you want to guess what happened?

The check never came. The commercial property was sold. He never got 1 penny. He lost it all. He had to quit working on his business and get another full time job. And he will never ever be able to start another business again. His wife has threatened him with divorce if he ever brings it up.

Listen to me when I say this. There is a non-stop supply of such stories. Prevent this from happening to you. Start small and scale up. Grow at your own comfortable pace.

Dealing with lawn care customers.

- **How other lawn care operators deal with customers to keep everyone happy.**

We asked a Gopher Forum member, "Have you ever run into finicky customers who complain after the landscape construction is completed that they don't like it and want it another way or simply want their money back?

What advise do you have for dealing with difficult customers?"

He said "my best advice is the more time you spend with the customer before the project, the less time you have to spend after. What I mean is if you spend as much time with the customer before starting the project, you will have a good idea of their needs/demands. It is a lot easier to iron problems out before starting the project then when everything is complete.

Now with this said, I still have challenging or more demanding customers regularly. One thing that you have to remember is the customer is the one paying for this service. You have to put yourself in their shoes...$10,000.00 for a patio, you bet I am going to get it the way I want.

If it is nearly impossible to satisfy a customer, I try putting the ball back in their court. For example...A set of steps. The customer wanted 8" rises and you gave them 6 1/2" rises without talking to them first. This would be your responsibility to fix the situation! Now if rise was never discussed (shame on you) you can work around this. Ask the customer what they are displeased with. They will provide you with an answer. You then ask them "Mr. or Mrs. Customer, if I make this modification to the steps, will you be pleased with the outcome of this project?" Nine times out of ten, you will get a satisfied customer this way because they had a chance to get everything out on the table that was bothering them. If you repair everything they ask, even though you know that it looks better with 6 1/2" rises etc... they have no recourse. However if you never bother to seek the problem, you can never remedy the situation.

Sometimes you have to lose money on a project to keep a customer happy. This is very frustrating to do. If however you leave that dissatisfied customer you are likely to get a bad name quickly. Someone will provide a friend, family member, neighbor, or colleague advice on NOT choosing a company rather than positive advice about a company. If a customer feels like they got "ripped off" of $10,000.00 they will tell everyone. Seems like everyone was talking about getting ripped off at the pump when it was $3.00 but when it is below $2.00 it seems to take a back stage is an example that comes to mind.

Just my two cents on customer satisfaction but what do I know...I am just a starving dirt farmer!"

We then asked, "have you found yourself learning more and more early warning signs when dealing with a customer? Do you do anything to pre-qualify them? Have you ever backed out of a project before you started because you felt the customer was going to be too difficult?"

Michael said "No, I do not pre-qualify! I used to judge but that lost me a few jobs! Never go by house size, car driven, color, race, religion etc! I have been taken on 2 jobs in my 10 years of business. Both jobs were customers who fit your stereotypical white collared wealthy business person. A small house should mean to you a smaller mortgage, meaning more money to spend on landscape. A more mid range car should mean smaller or not even having a car payment, which equals more money to spend on landscape.

There is such a thing as intuition. And your feeling of a customer should be very important but like I said before, the people I least suspected got me. So the moral of the story is get a good contract in place, get a solid deposit and clearly discuss payment terms before the project. Do not expect the customer to know them because it says so in the contract. Read it to them and explain it to them. Ask them if the understand the payment terms. Ask them if they have questions. Explain to them the payment forms you accept (credit card, check, cash, money order, debit card, gift card etc...)

A customer that typically ask about financing or if you take credit cards generally does not have the money to pay for the project in "liquid assets" or in a checking account. This does not have to be a red flag; however look more into their questioning.

Another key warning sign is a customer tells you how to do a project. This is a typical DIY homeowner. You have to be very up front and honest with this type of customer. Nicely explain to them that they hired you for your professional services and that is what you are going to deliver. You have developed processes over the years that have proven to be very effective and that is the way that the job will go. Basically you are telling them that if they know so much about this why they don't do it themselves."

Questions to ask new customers who call you.

When new potential customers call you, there are questions you can ask them to pre-screen them and find out if they will be the kind of customer you want.

Ask the caller if this is their first experience using a lawn care operator. If not, ask them why they are planning on switching. This will help you gain some insight into the customer. If may also help provide you with valuable information or throw up red flags. You might find out if the customer is simply a constant price shopper. These are customers you want to avoid.

Joe said "Another red flag is if they insist on specific pricing over the phone. If they are truly interested they would be happy to have a 'free lawn inspection' or at least a free quotation. If they are insisting on a price over the phone, they are probably just price hunting and will go with the lowest price... let 'em go!

Don't forget to ask where they heard of your business. And keep track throughout the year so that you know where your calls are coming from. This is valuable data!"

Chestin said "Asking questions right at the outset will definitely go a long way towards helping you understand your customers better. It will also help you provide a service they consider to be valuable.

If they're switching, asking them why they're switching will give you a good indication as to the areas you'll need to pay special attention to if you happen to land the account. After they've given you their reasons, tailor your sales message as best you can to highlight your experience, expertise, or service policies related to their concerns. Don't make any empty promises and always makes sure you follow through on any promises you do make.

If they're purchasing services for the first time, ask them what prompted them to buy. Again, their responses will give you good insight into what areas you should pay particular attention to. It will also help you understand potential customers that are very similar. Often times, the reasons they've decided to begin purchasing services will be the same reasons shared by others. Take note of those reasons and use them to your advantage.

Finally, as Joe mentioned, if you can tell someone's 'price shopping', don't waste your time. They'll end up being more trouble than they're worth and your time is much better spent finding and developing relationships with customers that appreciate your work for more than just the amount you charge. If you're competing on price alone, you're asking for more headaches, hassles, and hard-times than you know!"

Thank you letters to customers?

Andre asked for tips on thank you letters.

Joe responded by saying "the thank you letter is an important and often overlooked aspect of making your customers feel appreciated.

Thank you notes or letters can be delivered at anytime. For example:

- After a signing a new customer to a maintenance agreement
- At the end of a season
- After signing or completing a big job
- After they have referred someone else to your company
- Anytime you want to thank your customer or just remind them that you are still here

Thank you notes should be brief and to the point. Consider a card or postcard to say thanks. The note may be accompanied by a small gift in special circumstances however do not include marketing material. It would seem like you are trying to sell them something under the pretense of doing something nice. The purpose of the thank you note is to do a nice thing for the sake of doing it so leave out the flyers or other advertisements. That being said there is nothing wrong with following up after a couple of weeks with some promotional material.

The above information relates to a specific thank you note however always remember to thank you customers for their business is all your correspondence to them."

What should you include in your hand written thank you card?
How about something like this.

> *"Thank you for your business. I really appreciate it.*
> *Please keep in mind if you need to get in touch with me for*
> *any reason, please call. Also if you could, please pass on a*
> *few of my business cards to anyone you know who might*
> *need my services. I would be thankful for any referrals*
> *you could send my way.*
>
> *Sincerely,*
> *Joe"*

Ed: "Our company is a little to big to customize our marketing.
With 15 lawn care technicians and an average of 25 lawns per
technician, it would be difficult to keep track of.

I think making sure the customer is well informed on how your
company handles different situations would help with the
customer retention. In my welcome kit, I have tried to include
answers to every question they may have.

I started my welcome kits this past summer. Next month I will do
an analysis on the retention rate from the customers that received
a welcome kit to see if it really has any affect."

Steve: "Do you mean you include a general list of business
frequently asked questions? Like who to contact. How you bill
etc. Or do you mean more like lawn specific problem questions?"

Ed: "Both. It contains the frequently ask questions about how we
do business & answers about how much the lawn should be
watered, mowed, etc. Also answers about what to do after the

applications, and if they come across any problems with their lawns."

Chestin: "I can see how sending a personalized letter with specifics about the property could be very beneficial, but at the same time it's almost too much work.

I think Ed hit the nail on the head in the sense you want to create materials that are reusable and duplicable.

Consider sending out different thank you letters at different times of the year. Each one would contain something different that cements the relationship, reminds the customer of all the benefits they'll be receiving, and potentially even upsells or lets them know about additional services you offer as well.

Ultimately, it comes down to building a relationship with the customer and viewing them like a person, not a transaction. The instant they become simply a transaction is the instant they're on their way out the door as a customer. Especially in today's economy."

Ed: "That is a good point. I think I will look into doing that also. Maybe by sending them a survey to see if we have met their expectations so far, or to see if they have any questions we may be able to answer."

Steve: "How do you suggest coming up with a list of frequently asked questions, to answer?"

Chestin: "I always suggest sitting down and making a list of general questions. Ideally they're ones that come up frequently, but it could also include questions that we might think are extremely basic.

One thing to remember is that it's easy to assume people know the basics about what you do. In most cases however, people don't have the first idea so my rule of thumb is never assume anything."

So the next time you sign up a new lawn care customer, you will be well equipped to do the best you can to retain that customer for the long haul and make them feel appreciated and wanted.

How to come up with your lawn care customer base goals for next year?

If you are like most lawn care business owners, you want to see your business grow over time. How are you going to do this though? Do you have a plan? What are your lawn care customer base goals? That is the amount of base customers you want to be servicing weekly.

I asked this question on the Gopher Lawn Care Business Forum and got a great response I wanted to share with you.

Tim: "To develop a lawn care customer base goal, a lawn care business owner needs to start with time management, this is very important. How many customers can they handle in a normal work week and how eager are they. After they have the first season under their belt then they can analyze how many more customers they can handle. They can decide how fast they want to grow. This depends on the individual For me if I was to just do lawn cutting and basic light landscaping **I wouldn't want more than 30-40 full time lawn care customers.** This would leave me time to do mulch and other services for those customers and still have personal time. This would be an ample customer base for a 1 man business. If the one man show started with 15 full time customers, the next season he should set his goal to add at least 5 more full timers."

Steve: "How many customers should a lawn care operator then shoot for if they want to take on an employee? What kind of range would you suggest?"

Tim: "One of my friends in the lawn care industry has 135 customers with a mixture of commercial and residential. He has a 2-3 man lawn care crew, so counting him there are normally 4 men. They stay pretty busy yet he recently called me to do some mulch jobs for him because he was swamped.

I wouldn't do more than 35-40 lawns per one man crews. With a 2 man crew I would suggest between 90-100 lawn care customers if they are balanced commercial and residential. If most of the business is commercial or industrial, I would say it would be less because of the time constraints to mow larger properties and perform the other services offered. In the winter months if there isn't any snow plowing going on he keeps them busy scraping or doing odd jobs."

I hope this information helps you develop your lawn care customer base goals for next season.

New lawn care customer welcoming kit.

Are you giving all of your new lawn care customers a Welcoming Kit? If you aren't you should start doing it. This is something that can really help keep your customers from leaving you.

Things to include in your Lawn Care Customer Welcoming Kit folder.

- Welcoming Letter.
- Newsletter.
- Business Card.
- Mission statement.
- A list of your Frequently Asked Question's.
- List all the services you offer.
- A brochure on each major program you offer, like plant health care and bug barricade.
- Information on the supplementals you are currently promoting.
- A referral card to pass on to friends or family.

One of our forum members wrote, "I started these welcome kits to help the new lawn care customers understand who we are and what we have to offer. When researching our cancellation history I found that most of the canceled lawn care accounts had been canceled within the first 3-4 months. If they had been more informed from the beginning, maybe we could have saved the sale."

How to get 30% more lawn care customers?

I had a great conversation with Jeff, a lawn care business owner, on the Gopher Forum. He shared with us his insight on how he has been able to grow and what he uses to push himself to get more flyers out and meet more potential lawn care business customers.

Jeff: "I got 55 lawn care customers within 6 months of opening my lawn service full time last year and just finished a record cash season this Summer. Sometimes my lawn care customer total swells to 65, and last winter it dropped to 35, but it currently is about 55+.

In advertising, I use lawn care business flyers door to door, getting out as many as 800+ in one day. In this area, you get about 2 calls every 300 flyers. I pass out thousands of flyers. Then I also get referrals, that's probably 1 out of 5 customers. I also advertise in a local paper. A recent 4 week ad in this paper produced maybe 14 calls, and resulted in a few new customers, one of which was a much needed monthly contract. **So these three methods, flyers, referrals, and an ad in a popular local paper are how I get the customers.**

But an insider tip I learned from the TV show "The Apprentice" I would have to credit also. I watch any TV show that I could learn something about business from, so I watch The Apprentice and I noticed it was usually the team that pushed it, that won. So I adopted this in my efforts when passing out lawn care flyers, and time and time again I have seen it work. I will be out passing out lawn care flyers and feel like ending the effort (after all I'm the boss, I can quit when I want-right?) but I would pretend I was on The Apprentice and push onward distributing far more lawn care flyers so I could stay out of the boardroom, so to speak, and sure enough, I would get calls usually from the additional lawn care flyers I distributed. So this insight is key to building up a big list soon- push it!!!! Just pretend you'll have to stand in front of Donald Trump if your team loses, and that you may be fired, then really push it.

This insight has gotten me probably 30% of all my lawn care customers."

Steve: "Do you do anything to promote referrals? Do you have any suggestions on how to get them?"

Jeff: "To answer the referral question, I do stuff like give a customer a thank you card, thanking them for their continual business, and I'll include a business card asking them to refer anyone they know to me, to give them the extra business card. But I find most referrals come naturally from the customers voluntarily, because they like the good work you do for them and want to share your service."

Shane: "You are smart to hand out your lawn care business flyers yourself. At my previous lawn care job, my boss's major problem was he let the lawn care employees distribute flyers unsupervised. I'm pretty sure they were playing X Box and trashing the flyers. If you distribute lawn care flyers, always make sure that you are present to supervise or help flyer yourself. You are the only one that ensures that the lawn care business flyers get on the doors.

Also make sure you are answering your phone. Why have a

marketing plan if you are never going to answer your phone, return phone calls or check your voicemail? Now when I give a bid or give out a business card I always tell the customer to call me and write my cell phone number on the back, so they feel special."

Find out why a customer is canceling service and resolve it.

When a lawn care customer calls to cancel service there are some things you should do to try and keep them. If you can't keep them, try to find out why they are leaving.

The customer is canceling for a reason. They may not want to tell you the reason face to face or on the phone but they just might tell you in a letter. Why not make it your policy to send them a cancellation letter and keep track of the reasons why your lawn care customers cancel your service. It will help you improve parts of your lawn care business you are not seeing but the lawn care customer does. Find out what is wrong with your business. Find out why they are canceling. Then strive to improve that section of your lawn care business so no further lawn care business customers cancel.

In a letter, tell the customer you are saddened to see them go. Let the customer know you strive to provide the highest level of service and in order to continually provide that, you need their help.

Ask the customer if they would please respond to your survey as to why they decided to leave.

- Did they notice an improvement to their property since they hired your company to provide lawn service?

- Would they use your services again in the future?

- Would they refer your business to friends or family?

- How would they rate your service on a 1 – 10 scale?

- Is there a specific reason they decided to cancel service

and if so what was it?

- What is their opinion on how you can improve?

- Would they hire you again in the future if you were able to improve upon the issue that caused them to cancel service?

- Could you call the customer to discuss this?

These questions should give you a good heads up as to what went wrong and how you can go about fixing the problem so it won't happen again in the future and cost you more customers.

Steve: "I think this is something most small lawn care businesses miss. They never find out why a customer is canceling. When a customer cancels with you do you ask them on the phone why? Or does a sales staff member talk to them?
Do you ask them any specific questions as to why they are canceling and do you offer any inducements to try and keep them with you for a little longer? How do you keep track of this? Does your staff have a check list of questions to ask?"

Bob: "When a lawn care customer calls in to cancel, we always ask if there is a specific reason. We always try to satisfy them or resolve the issue. If for some reason they still cancel, I send them a cancel letter along with a small survey asking more specific questions. A lot of times the customer does not tell us the real reason when we are talking to them over the phone, but they will tell us on the survey. During early spring when the weather is more difficult to work with, our lawn care technicians can use this information to try to call the customer back up to gain their business again. Also when we receive the survey back, one of the managers that can handle the issue will give the customer a call to talk to them about it and try to resolve the issue."

Have you found yourself in a situation where you recently sign up a new lawn care customer only to have them cancel shortly there after? Did you ever wonder why that is the case?

It's called buyer's remorse Let's take a look into this phenomenon and what to do to prevent it from happening.

Chestin wrote "One comment about the lawn care customer cancellation rates. It's pretty typical in ANY business to see the majority of your cancels refunds occur very shortly after the purchase. It's called 'buyer's remorse'.

One of the things I suggest is to **send a customer 'stick' letter/card shortly after the first visit** or two, reminding them about your great service, why you're such a great VALUE, and of all the BENEFITS they'll be getting. You might even consider including in your 'welcome packet' (which is another FANTASTIC idea I recommend to all my clients as well) a customer survey asking what they're hoping to receive and/or the reasons they hired you. Consider including a postage paid envelope to make it easy for them to return, but when they do, send them a 'thank you' card with some type of gift card or other 'goodie' as a way of letting them know you appreciate their feedback."

This is a great way to improve upon your lawn care customer retention. Sending a card or survey in the beginning of service is well worth the effort when you consider how long you might keep that lawn care customer around for.

How to collect on overdue accounts.

When you are running your lawn care business, you will inevitably run into a customer who decides they aren't going to pay you What do you do when a lawn care customer refuses to pay their bill? How should a lawn care business owner handle this? Let's look into this.

Amy: "Hello everyone! I'm sure it's happened to most of us…a customer that wants the garden weeded and then decides that her day lilies weren't trimmed just right and decides to not pay for the services rendered.

How do you get that person to pay for services that has been performed? Obviously you discontinue your services, but what about the past due amount? I have 2 lawn care accounts under $750.00 At this point, they're 8 weeks late."

Steve: There is a free letter in our lawn care customer letter section on the Gopher Forum you can download and edit to your use. It basically goes like this. Remember, to pass this letter by your attorney first before you send it. Add what you want to it and then send it out certified return receipt requested.

Dear Mr. Defendant,

You had hired me on Jan 15th 200X to cut down your tree. I have since cut down the tree and removed it from your property. As per our verbal agreement I am requesting to be paid $X00.00 for my services. Contact me if you have any further questions.

*If I do not hear from you within 30 days from the receipt of this
letter I will file a petition with small claims court in XXXXXX
County.*

*I look forward to working with you toward a resolution of this
matter.*

Very truly,

Your Name

If you still don't hear from them, you can file a claim in small
claims court. But sending out such a letter will most likely show
them you are serious about collecting.

Ben: "Go by there every day and knock on her door. Eventually
she will get tired of you coming by and pay you . I learned this
when I was a collection manager. You may feel like a jerk at first,
but then, who's the one that wont pay? Her. It really does work."

Amy: "Thanks for the sample collection letter you posted, I was
paid. That's one deadbeat down and 1 to go! It was a small
victory and a boost to my self esteem."

Steve: "That is great news! Tell us what you did to get paid. I am
sure a lot of new lawn care business owners are reading this,
wondering what steps you took to get success."

Amy: "First, I called the Small Claims Court in my County and gathered information on starting a small court claim. How much to file, how much for the Sheriff to serve papers, etc. Then, I gathered my information regarding my deadbeat client; like the dates we performed lawn & garden maintenance and filled in the blanks. I stressed she had 5 days after the receipt of the letter to settle her bill. If not, then I will file a claim against her for theft of services.

I went to the post office and sent the letter registered mail. 3 days later, I received her payment in full. I ran to the bank and deposited the check; hoping she didn't put a stop payment on it! Accompanying her check was a little nasty note stating that she was the one who fired us, but that doesn't excuse her nonpayment.

Here's the lawn care business debt collection letter format that I used. I removed the personal information and others who use it can just fill in the blanks appropriately.

Dear deadbeat:

You had hired ABC Company on (insert date) to perform garden maintenance at 3 week intervals, starting this day. At the same time, you hired us for lawn maintenance at an agreed price of $$, starting this day. Since then, I've performed garden maintenance per our contract on this day and lawn maintenance was performed on the following dates. Payment terms per our contract are due upon completion. Payments for the services listed above are now due immediately. Despite several phone calls to you to collect payment, you have stated on 3 separate occasions that your payment is in the mail. Since I have not received payment to date, your services were terminated by ABC Company on said date, due to theft of services.

*As per our contract, I am requesting to be paid $$$
for our services......*

Steve: "Thank you for sharing your experience with us."

Dealing with employees.

- **How to know when the time is right to make the jump to hiring employees.**

Cliff asked the following question: "At what point did you decide to take on your first employee? Was it determined by revenue, time constraint or did you set a specific profit amount that would determine time to add help?"

Joe answered "the decision to take on employees is a big one.

I took on a part time helper in my first year and in my second year I took on a full time employee who turned out to be with me for the entire time I operated by business.

On the one hand, employees mean extra work and expenses so the inclination might be to stay small as long as possible. However, the game of landscape maintenance is one best played with two people. In other words a two person team is more efficient that one for most residential settings. So, my advice is that even if you intend to stay small, get big enough to keep you and a helper busy.

The first signal that you may need help is quite simply that you are very busy and your phone is still ringing with new work. If that is your situation then you should calculate the cost of hiring a helper.

> 1) Look at your profit and loss data. If you are not profiting without an employee, hiring one will not help you.

> 2) Add up all the monthly costs that go with hiring an employee and don't forget to include the 'hidden' costs like Workers' Compensation and matching of certain source deductions.

> 3) Determine if it is feasible to take on staff based on your current revenue and profit.

It may be that you can only afford a part time helper until you build your business some more. It would also depend on how fast you are able to grow and how difficult it is too find work. You may be pleasantly surprised if you take on a helper that you get enough work to keep you both busy."

Tom said "If you are getting to the point where you need help, then my suggestion would be to hire on someone that would work 2 to 3 days a week on your most busy days. That not only gives you time to train the person, but the ability to get more customers. Then you can make the person full time.

There are a lot of downsides though, and I know first hand experience about. Here are some things to think about

1. When you hire on someone, you open up a whole new can of worms. Insurance, payroll, liability, etc. It will now cost you more money to do the same work that you did before. Don't think that by having another employee all jobs will go faster. The only jobs where it will go faster is with larger properties.

2. What happens if you hire on an employee, and grow to 100 customers? But before you know it, that employee quits, and now you are stuck taking care of 100 properties yourself, before you can find someone else to hire and train.

3. Expect the quality of work to probably go down. Your quality is going to be a lot higher than your employees. To employees, their work is only a paycheck. Employees that work for the green industry and are entry level really could care less about the company.

4. Expect a high turnover rate with entry level employees. Before you know it, you may even see them as your competition

5. Have systems in place and regulations. You have to set ground rules up front with the employee, and don't budge on them. Once you budge, they know that they can take advantage of you.

I have had it before where I had one employee all the way up to two crews working. I went back to working solo though because the profit margin was really low with employees, they were a constant headache, and the quality of work was not 100% of what I wanted. Will I ever go back to employees? Maybe. But definitely not in the next 2 years."

How to make the jump from one crew to two.

Jon wrote to ask "How do you suggest expanding from one two-man crew to more?"

Joe responded by saying "The jump from a one two-man crew to more crews can be a challenge. Consider these points as you think about making that move.

1) Take a close look at your numbers. Have your accountant also look at your books. Are you profiting with your one crew? If you are not profiting with one crew, hiring more crews will not help you.

2) If you decide you are definitely ready for more staff the big question is how to transition since you are bound to go through a period where you are too busy for one crew but not busy enough for two. Here are a couple of suggestions:

a) What I did was hire a third person for my existing crew. That way we could get our jobs done faster and fit more customers into our day. When you reach the breaking point for the three-man crew then you can hire one more person and create a new two-man crew.

b) Another suggestion is to hire part timers to work 2, 3 or 4 days a week. This is less desirable because you will have the crew's vehicle and equipment sitting idle for some of the time and that's a waste of resources. However, if you are growing fast enough and can build up this crew to full time in short order (say a few months) then it is a fair strategy.

If you are doing things right and your market is good you will probably find that, whichever method you use, you will grow into a new crew fairly quickly."

What keeps your lawn care business small?

One of our forum members created a post to show off part of his fleet of lawn care business trucks. In his post, I had a great opportunity to learn a little about what stops most small lawn care businesses from ever getting themselves up to his size. I hope some of these questions and answers can really help you push forwards farther.

Steve: "With all these trucks, I would think you would be in a great position to have insight into why you feel the majority of lawn care business owners never get to the size you are at now?

What keeps most of them small?"

Mark: "Everyone has different reasons, but here are a few that come to mind.

> 1. They spend too much money on equipment, trucks, etc., before the business can support the costs. If you notice, all of my trucks are older but paid for. A nice new truck looks pretty and all, but I can do the same thing and only spend 1/10th of the cost.

> 2. Greed is a big killer. You must pay your helpers a decent wage to keep them. My lawn guys average $20+ an hour. I don't have the employee turn over that most do. My workers are paid a percentage of the job, so the more work the get, the more they make. This allows me to grow without worries of help being there.

3. They never dedicate themselves. They do the lawn work as a supplemental income and have another job too. With the security of the "day job", many won't strive for growth."

Steve: "Do you have any suggestions on how a lawn care business owner should structure their employee percentage incentives?"

Mark: "Foreman 20%, Crew 15%. As an example, say you have a 3 man crew handling a yard that is being charged $35 per cut.

The foreman would get ($35 x 20%) = $7
and each crew member get ($35 x 15%) = $5.25 each."

Incentives to get employees to sell more?

Scott suggested "There is no one magic bullet for quick success in this business. You need to work many different angles simultaneously. Get your employees into this as well. Offer them an incentive to sign up new customers. How about a $50.00 bonus for each customer who signs up for a yearly contract?"

Another Gopher Forum member posted his new business cards and they didn't have a his name on them, unlike most normal business cards. I asked why and got some great insight from him that you might be able to utilize as well.

Steve: "Jim can you tell us the advantage / disadvantage to not having your name on the business card?"

Jim: "Well part of our bonus structure promotes our foreman to bid jobs and actually become salesman. This eliminates the need to have individual cards for everyone. Plus we are growing quite rapidly, and I don't want everyone knowing I am the owner.

People automatically assume that since I am the owner, I can magically fix everything. Billing issues are the secretary's job. On the job issues...ie...gates left open...(they do need to be handled, but I force my foreman to take responsibilities. If a customer calls the office to mention the gate issue my secretary calls the foreman and not me."

Steve: "That is fascinating and I think a very smart move, it must be cost effective!

Getting to your bonus structure, would this mean if your foreman is out on a job and the customer says they need a new retaining wall, your foreman can create a bid on the spot to do the job? Or how does that work? How are they trained to know how to bid?"

Jim: "In a situation like that, they would fill out an estimate request sheet in their daily route book with their name on it. My secretary sets up the estimate. Upon receiving complete payment, he or she get their bonus. It ranges between 2 and 4% of the total job not including tax. So if it's a $10,000 job, he can stand to make up to $400.00. Not bad huh?? And it's all factored in to the numbers of the estimate so it doesn't cost me a dime. For lawn estimates, they get the amount of the first cut as a bonus."

What are you training your lawn care employees to do?

When you hire employees for your lawn care business, they are on the front lines. The impressions they make with the public and your customer base is going to do a lot to effect whether your business survives or fails. So think about these things when you are considering what you are training your lawn care employees.

Do you have a sales manager for your lawn care business? Bob does and he wrote "I am in the process of hiring a sales manager to where I will be able to work with them on contacting homeowners associations. I also want them to go to other businesses that could be connected to us, like lawn mower repair shops, real estate agents, builders, mortgage companies, etc. to work with them on sending us referrals."

What about your mowing crews? Are you training them to be the first to say hi to people while they are out and about? This is very important. They are ambassadors of your business. They need to come across as approachable and friendly.

Bob wrote "My lawn care crews are trained to look for problems in the lawn. If the customer is not home, they will write a note on their invoice recommending a specific product/treatment. Our lawn care technicians always go to the door and knock before doing any treatment. If the customer is home they will see if there is anything specific they want them to look at."

Keep these ideas in mind as your lawn care business grows and you look for ways to help your staff bring in more business. They are on the front lines and they are in the best position to offer suggestions to upsell the lawn care customer which ultimately will bring in more profits.

What every lawn care employee should be taught.

Do you ever wonder how much training your employees should be given? For instance, do they need to be trained on how to change belts? Or is that just something that would be too much for most of them?"

Tom: "All employee's should be trained on every minor mechanical repair detail you can do in the field. Change belts, fixing flats, adjusting the drive alignments, changing oil, filters and keeping the equipment greased and blades sharpened. Most of this is VERY minor stuff and if not trained on it, they should be able to figure it out in minimal time.

Not only should they be trained on equipment repairs they should also be trained on how to properly operate the equipment they are using, to prevent unnecessary repairs and equipment brake downs. This includes all equipment, proper use of string trimmers, hand operated tools, right along with the mowing equipment. You would be surprised at how many people THINK they know how to run commercial grade equipment and it's a BIG surprise to them they don't.

I think every lawn care business owner should properly train there employees on how YOU want it done and used Everyone has there own way of doing things and I am one of those guys that want it done a certain way. Here is why; I have serviced EVERY customer multiple times and have tried different ways to do each of these customers' yards and have already figured out the fastest and best way to get it done.

So in a nut shell YES I'm a firm believer in proper training in every aspect, EVERY NEW GUY rides shotgun with me before I send them out with any other crew. This way I feel better about other crews servicing my client."

How many lawns are you cutting with a 3 man crew?

A great question was posted on the Gopher Forum and it asked how many lawns can a 3 man crew can cut?

Chuck responded by saying: "I currently run a 3 man crew (myself & 2 helpers). One truck, one trailer, 2 mowers, 3 trimmers, 3 blowers, edgers etc....

Typically on a 10,000 sf residential lot, we pull up, one man on each of the 2 mowers, one does front & one side, other does rear & other side. 3rd guy line trims & edges. 1st 2 guys done blow off while the 3rd closes up the trailer.

We are in & out in 10-12 minutes, 15 including drive time (yes clustering the jobs together & tightening your route helps the bottom line a ton, but this takes time!)

I average 28-30 properties a day, currently running 4 full days (9-10 hours per day) if all goes well with no breakdowns, snags, or rain delays."

> **Q:** What is more efficient a two man lawn care crew or a 3 man lawn care crew?

Chuck: "I anticipate next season expanding & adding a 2nd truck, & running each with 2 men on it. I've found 2 man teams to be more profitable, 3 is faster but eats up profit as guy #3 adds slightly more production than his payroll expense. I just can't swing another full rig right this minute & 2 guys can't keep up so the 3rd is a necessary expense for me right now."

So ultimately as you expand, you might want to scale up from a 2 man crew to a 3 man crew. Then hire a 4th employee and create two (2 man crews).

Insights on hiring employees for your lawn care business.

This is a great discussion I wanted to share with you about hiring lawn care employees form this post at the Gopher Lawn Care Forum.

Steve: "What is tougher, hiring your first employee or having to hire and manage a second crew? Which was the bigger jump for you, do you feel? A lot of small business owners get stuck at both points and I was wondering what advice you had on this."

Rich: "I do not really think that I struggled with either. If I had to pick one I would say it would have been probably, hiring and managing the second crew. Although, even hiring your first employee can be somewhat difficult. The best advise I can give is first off you will never find an employee that is going to have the standards that you personally as the owner of the business would have, the common interest is not the same. You will however find a few great employees.

The hardest thing for me as I am sure with many is the hiring and managing of the second crew, primarily this is because the loss that you feel of being able to provide your customers with the superior level of service that you would personally provide. This however is going to be difficult, (a necessary evil that you must overcome) in order for you to grow the business you will have to (trust your employees, at least to some degree) and learn to be a good delegator.

The other common mistakes that I have made is never hire for an immediate spot out of pure necessity. Be cautious of hiring immediate friends, and especially family members. Sometimes those can be the worst mistakes for you to make. The key to finding good employees is to always be looking and to always be interviewing because you never know when that (perfect) employee may come around."

Steve: "How do you suggest doing this? Should you always be advertising that you are hiring?

If you found someone you thought would be good and didn't really have a spot for them at the moment, would you hire them anyway and make a spot? "

Rich: "About advertising, for hiring or open positions. If you have a shop (store front) you could always have a sign up to draw in potential applicants, you could also have a referral program for your employees (refer a friend). I don't mean to necessarily advertise in news papers that obviously can be expensive. The other thing is when out and about in my day if I see someone anywhere working that I feel would possibly be a good fit maybe offer them a business card and ask them to call you if they ever consider a different type of work field. (I am not saying go to your competitors) go to the gas stations, convenience stores, pharmacy stores, restaurants like Wendy's, McDonalds, etc, you would be surprised.

In the past some of my best workers came from restaurants and had never done lawn care ever before. Also, when I used to be in management retail chain and Big Box stores I personally was recruited this way for some of the top companies in the world.

(ex.) one store offered me a co-store manager position to start, my own store within 6 months and I was working at a competitor at the time. Recruited by a District Manager and Super Center Manager out price comparing and head hunting.

I don't think that I would hire just to get that person if I already had a great crew, but if I did not have that great of a crew you bet, I would make a spot and move into when someone else cut their own throat and dropped the ball and I would have a trained replacement on staff already."

Steve: "That is pretty fascinating stuff! So you actually were offered a job while you were at work! Were you blown away by that? It makes you wonder how often this goes on!

In the past when you hired someone that was working at a restaurant, were they your waiter? And then maybe you asked them if they ever considered working in lawn care? Or how would you suggest approaching the topic? "

Rich: "Yes I was working when I was approached by the competitor's management and said that they would really like to discuss opportunities with me. They said they had been in a few times and were very impressed with my overall work ethic and management style. I told them I would not discuss any opportunities with them while I was working they proceeded with giving me their card and they called me the next day and were persistent for me to come in so my next off day I did go in to speak with the district manager at his office. They offered me a great position, however I declined to accept the job do to a serious family medical situation. This was one of three head hunters that approached me just while I worked at this store for a short period of time.

To answer your other question, when I would ask people, they could have been the waiter, waitress, cashier, host, anybody who I thought may have had the overall customer service qualities that I would look for. You can teach almost anybody a trade or a skill, However obvious customer service skills and the way one presents themselves is a talent they must master on their own.

Conversation would just be brought up in a general friendly talk, no pressure by any means, maybe a compliment on their quality of work or by the way they presented themselves."

Why lawn care businesses fail.

A look inside how a lawn care business failed.

We don't often get a chance to look inside a lawn care business after it fails but there is a lot to learn from the experience. Most of all, we want to know why it failed. What did the owner do or not do that attributed to the demise of his lawn care business?

Mike wrote, "I am 21 years old and have 2 years of a college education complete in working towards a business management degree. My education has been temporarily suspended while I get this lawn care business up off the ground. I have always been told that I am very business and entrepreneur oriented, and consider myself to have some business sense for my age.

Previously to starting this lawn care company I was the manager of another lawn and landscape company in my town. This lawn care company is now defunct. This past February the owner came and told me he was going to liquidate his lawn care company. This was a bombshell to me because he had led me to believe I had a future with his company and maybe even an ownership opportunity. He did offer me his residential lawn care accounts free of charge. I felt this was the least he could do. He agreed to send all of the lawn care customers letters explaining the transition, and agreed to help me get started. However, I haven't heard from him since, and he never sent the letters.

I pressed forward and talked to as many lawn care customers as I could, and was still able to pick up some. I picked up some others on my own by flyering and bought some accounts from a competitor mid-season. All in all I would consider my first year in business to be a success. I have learned a lot."

Steve: "What do you think attributed to the liquidation of that company? What do you feel you learned from the experience?"

Mike: "First of all I said that it was a bombshell that he was going to liquidate in my previous post. This is partly untrue. I should have seen the writing on the wall, as it was all over the place, but I was 100% committed to turning this lawn care company around and making it work. Also, as recently as December (He liquidated in February) we had meetings discussing the future of the company and my role with it. Never was liquidation mentioned. Three major contributing factors led to him having to liquidate his lawn care business:

> **Money Management (Debt):** This guy had more debt than you could shake a stick at. I never have seen anything like it. He financed his entire business on credit cards and used credit cards to run his business. He also never made smart purchases. We had 7 lawn care trucks 5 of which had valid registration and license plates. We never used more than two in a day. 3 of these lawn care trucks were nice or decent and the other two were junk. Why wouldn't get rid of them?
>
> Why? I'm still asking myself. Also we had a shop full

of lawn care equipment that never got used. We were primarily a lawn mowing company with some landscaping, and a snow removal operation in the winter. For instance. This guy had probably over $3,000 in tree trimming equipment. He had everything you could imagine. You could scale a California Redwood with this crap.

In the third seasons I was there we maybe did two tree jobs. Neither of them required more than chainsaws and trucks. Ridiculous. Also with all this debt and credit cards eager to spend money on he never purchased a skid steer or compact utility loader which we were in dire need of. In the time I was there we spent so much money renting Bobcats we could have bought a damn good used one if not a new one. He wouldn't break down and make that purchase, or at least purchase a dingo or something.

Equipment Maintenance: He did no lawn care equipment maintenance whatsoever. I did the best I could to maintain his lawn care equipment when I came on, but most of it was already trashed. He had two commercial lawn mowers with less than 3000 hours on them that were just ruined. He never greased them or did the required maintenance. They burned oil etc.

His philosophy was all commercial engines burn oil. BULL HOCKEY. I purchased a new commercial mower and have put a lot of hours on it and it has yet to burn a ounce of oil. I have done all routine maintenance religiously. That is the only difference.

Also, in this lawn care business things happen. Things break. Things will need fixed from time to time. Whenever something needed to be fixed, 9 times out of 10 it was fixed improperly, not fixed at all, fixed halfway, or jerry rigged in some kind of way. Duct tape was his best friend. For this upcoming season he was going to need to drop a lot of money on equipment when all of it was prematurely destroyed, he had extended all of his credit and had spent all of the cash paying creditors. SCREWED.

Communication: This is one of the major keys to business success, and he ignored it. He failed to communicate with his lawn care customers and he failed to communicate with his lawn care employees. He had to go back to work full time at a local aircraft plant to pay creditors. That is the primary reason I was running his business. There would be weeks when I wouldn't even talk to him or him call me. I had a company credit card in my pocket. I went out did the work, sold a job or two, managed the employees, bought what we needed to operate and went home.

Often times when I would call him to give him a report on the events of the day he would act as if I was bothering him so I eventually just left it up to him to get a hold of me. Often times when we would communicate it would be over a case of beer at the shop. Nothing was ever serious. When I started calling his customers to let them know that A. he wasn't showing up this season and B. I was if they would give me a chance. I was flabbergasted by what one customer told me. This lawn care customer lived in a neighborhood where we typically did not do leaf removal, but his yard had more leaves than others. He said, " I probably called seven times last fall requesting a leaf cleanup, and not one of my calls was returned." I apologized and informed him that I had not been notified either. He was not at all surprised. He said that he had already found somebody else for the season and wished me luck. What could I say?

The story was similar with many of his lawn care customers.

Needless to say this lawn care business was doomed, so it is probably a good thing that he liquidated. I did learn a lot from this guy. Mostly how not to run a lawn care business. I could talk your head off about this guy, but that's pretty much the gist of it."

Steve: "What do you think got him into most of that debt? Do you know any history on how he got started in the lawn care business or why? Did he have any background? What do you think you will do differently from him?"

Mike: "As I said, 3 of these lawn care business trucks were decent and 2 were junk. We never really used more than 2 in any given day, but we did run 4 snow plows in the winter. 1 of these junk trucks was 2 wheel drive. We used it as our salt-sand truck, but it was useless with a plow on it. I was trying to get him to sell these two junk trucks and buy 1 nicer one that was 4 wheel drive and more functional.

His equipment replacement policy was simple. He didn't have one. He finally broke down and bought 2 new trimmers and a new push mower towards the end of last mowing season. The only reason he did this, was if he didn't we weren't going to be in operation. Consequently the trimmers were not broke in properly, because they had to be immediately thrown into service.

First, what got him into most of that debt? I'm not 100% certain. There were several mitigating factors, I'm sure. Like I said before, he made many unwise purchases. Most of these were financed by debt. He would realize that it was stupid and then go make another purchase to fix it financed by debt. It was just a compounding snow-ball effect. That is the way debt works. If you let it get a hold of you, it is going to snowball out of control. What is so ironic, is this guy isn't dumb. He graduated magna cum laude with a degree in economics from a ivy league school. He's a genius in a lot of aspects. A lot of times I thought he was almost too smart for his own good. It's amazing that he amassed such a large amount of debt with an education like that.

Yes, he did have a background in the industry. Him and a partner started out push mowing 40 lawn care mowing accounts about 8 years ago. What's sad is that 8 years later when he liquidated he only had about 75 lawn care mowing accounts. He just didn't grow enough to sustain his business structure. He had his business structured to be a full service, growing, lawn and landscape business, and he just couldn't sustain it without growth.

What am I doing/going to do different from him? A lot to say the least. I did start my lawn care business with a loan, but I made sure that it was one that the business could easily pay off. I have one company credit card, as opposed to his 10. I have only used this card when I have absolutely needed to. I use my cash in the bank when at all possible and avoid using my credit unless it is urgent or an emergency. Also, I know a thing or two about money, but not near as much about it as my Dad.

I have sort of brought him on as a C.F.O. type of figure to help manage the company finances. This was an excellent decision, and has definitely saved us some headaches.

Secondly, I perform all lawn care equipment maintenance religiously. All the maintenance charts were taken out of the lawn care equipment owners manuals, put on to spreadsheets, and posted in the shop. All of my trimmers, and blowers are serviced every 100 hours. Also, I plan to replace all the equipment every three seasons. Including vehicles. Another good rule to follow is try to replace at least one piece of equipment each season. For instance, I plan on replacing my hand held blower with a second back pack blower before next season. This is a good way to grow your equipment fleet as you grow your business and also keep things in good shape. Also, don't purchase equipment until you need it. For example, I did not purchase a chain saw this year until I sold my first tree job.

Thirdly, I communicate with all my lawn care customers and employees regularly. Talk to your employees daily, even if you get rained out. Always check your phone, and return phone calls. Check your voice mail. This guy never checked his voice mail. If your on a customer's property and you see them outside, take a minute, stop what you are doing and reach out to the customer. If nothing else just give a friendly hello or how are you doing.

Fourth, I market my lawn care business which he didn't do. We have signs on our truck. He didn't until his last year in biz. We flyer like crazy and we have a plan for growth. Those who fail to plan, plan to fail."

Don't damage the customer's lawn.

Have you ever found yourself cutting lawns and noticing after you cut the lawn, the tips of the grass blades are turning brown? You need to learn as much as you can about lawn care because the last thing you want to do is make the lawn look worse after you service it.

Frank: "I was wondering if anyone can help me out! I'm fairly new to the commercial end of the lawn care business. I've cut grass all my life but, it was for family. Now that I'm wanting to do it for a living I'm very serious about it. My question is when I cut the grass the top blades of grass turn brown. I have replaced my old mower blades with new gator blades and sharpened them before installing them. Can anyone help me out?"

Chuck: "Either A) your cutting the grass WAY TO LOW & need to raise the deck.

or

B) your lawn mower doesn't have the horsepower to be running gator blades. If your lawn mower is bogging down & the blades are moving too slow it will tug at the grass & rip it rather than just making a clean cut.

I would venture to say if your new at this…. It's probably A

Most homeowners scalp the hell out of their own lawns, mostly because they think it will go longer between cuts that way. Try raising the deck."

Frank: "Thanks for the reply! My main mower is a 48″ rider with a hp 17hp engine. My deck height is set at 2 3/4. I'm baffled."

Chuck: "Like I was saying…. raise your lawn mower deck. I don't know where you are located or what types of turf your having trouble with but I run most bahai lawns here with my decks no lower than 3.5″ some higher than that. St. Augustines & floritam I usually service between 4.25″- 4.5″.

Raise your lawn mower deck up & try it, It will look nicer, grow healthier, & be easier on your equipment."

Wasting money on ineffective ad designs.

If you find that ads you create to promote your lawn care business are not drawing new prospects, you need to re-evaluate how you are advertising. Know that your competitors are.

Matt recently posted a lawn care business ad he placed in a local magazine in our Gopher Lawn Care Business for review.

Here is what Chestin from Lawn Care Marketing Magic had to say about the ad. "While I know it's what everyone would expect to see in a magazine, that in itself is part of the problem. Most of today's marketing is ineffective. Here are the critical elements that should be included in EVERY piece of marketing you send out:"

1. **A benefit laden, attention grabbing headline**
2. You have less than 2 seconds to grab your prospects attention and unfortunately, your company name isn't enough. It's got to be something that promised some type of benefit or a solution to a problem they're having.
3. **Talk benefits, benefits, benefits**
4. Simply listing the services you offer doesn't really tell them how they'll benefit by hiring you. You've got to paint a picture for them and help them visualize how their life will be easier because of your service.
5. **Present some kind of valuable offer**
6. People are natural procrastinators and unless you give

them a reason to act, they won't. Yes, the 'Free Estimates' is an offer but everyone expects that these days so there's really nothing that makes people stop and think, "DANG, I've got to have that!"

7. Present them with an offer that will get them up off of the couch RIGHT NOW.

8. **Create urgency that motivates them to action**

9. Again, people are procrastinators and unless you give them a reason to respond right now, they won't. Doing things like limiting the number of packages available or attaching a deadline to an offer are good ways to create some urgency.

10. **Use 3rd party proof**

11. You did a GREAT JOB with this one by including the 'Before & After' photos in your ad. Testimonials are another great way to use 3rd party proof in your marketing.

12. **Present some kind of risk reversal**

13. People nowadays are skeptical and afraid of being taken for a ride so by including some type of risk reversal you make it easier for them to respond. Saying things like 'Satisfaction Guaranteed' or throwing in bonuses or premiums help your prospects feel safe when buying from you.

14. **Include a powerful call to action**

15. Unfortunately, you can't assume people know what they need to do, you've got to tell them in very specific terms. 'Pick up the phone and call us today' or 'Log onto our website at...' are good examples.

Now consider these great insights the next time you are putting together an ad to promote your lawn care business.

Not varying your direct mail campaign to address customer concerns.

Are you sending out the same piece of direct mail multiple times per year to the same area? Well our friend Tom made a good point here in the Gopher Lawn Care Business Forum that your lawn care business direct mail pieces can actually vary quite a bit if you pay attention to the needs of your potential lawn care customers depending on the area they live in. I asked Tom about his direct market mailings.

Steve: "If you could put together your dream marketing campaign concept what would you do differently?"

Tom: "As far as Direct Mail: I would target in on a specific area every week to 2 weeks. Not concentrate on the WHOLE metro area. I would take it one zip code at a time. Analyze the needs in each area and focus my mail pieces on them. I would concentrate my efforts on tightening the routes to help make the techs more efficient. Currently we cover about 70 zip codes. Out of that, 20 of them have a good to decent penetration rate. We could make it even better by focusing on it. I would rotate focusing on each area about 3 - 4 times a year."

Steve: "What kinds of things are you thinking about that could differ from area to area? How much could one zip code area's needs differ from another? What kinds of things are you thinking about?"

Tom: "For example: In the NE part of the city the ground is mostly a Sandy Loam. In the SW part it is Clay. Just like in any city there are areas where the homes are more high class. Those areas normally have more to their landscaping. We could offer a special on Plant Health Care. Each area has something distinctive about them, so I would focus on that quality. On the east side the homes are older and smaller. On the North side they are expanding and new subdivisions are popping up all the time. Each area has more of one type of grass than the other.

We could put a focus in the Spring on Bermuda Hydroseeding for the area where Bermuda grass is most popular. In the Fall we could focus on the Fescue Hydroseeding for the area where Fescue is most popular."

It is amazing how specific your direct marketing can get. Experiment with these ideas and try sending out different kinds of mailings.

Not talking to your customers to see if you can utilize their services.

Matt wrote us on the Gopher Lawn Care Business Forum about an interesting situation he had when talking to a local marketing company he serviced. He was initially looking for some marketing help to get the word out about his lawn care business. Here is what Matt wrote us.

Matt: "I went into her office a while back getting prices on things such as advertising and marketing help. They offer many advertising services such as pens, direct mailing postcards, business cards, and more. I came back in a few months later, she had said she was getting ready to do the Fall / Winter issue of her Home Builders Magazine, and asked if I were interested in a trade of a 1/2 page ad, because we don't keep up with our home yard.

The magazine ad is worth $500 on a 4 month cycle. So I can just cut her lawn bi-weekly at $50 a service for 5 months, her lawn is probably a quarter acre. I can use my 60in mower in her yard, probably total time there, 20 minutes. The house is in a good neighborhood, I can probably gain yards off her yard, I already do some homes in there anyway, so it's not hurting nothing. She had said the magazines fly off the shelves, which is a true fact, because I see them in the stores all the time full and not full, and sometimes gone. The magazines are free to the public to grab

She gave me advice on my ad and said "YOU DO NOT WANT YOUR AD TO LOOK BUSY," meaning too much information will hurt you. Make it look simple, clean, and crisp

The pictures on the ad are fall clean-up pics from last year, before and after.

She also designed my new logo at no charge She and I agreed to have bright colors so it can stand out.

We also added a "Mention this Ad for 5% off," coupon so I can know I am getting hits off of it.

She said to put my name on the ad so they know who they will be talking to before they call."

So the moral of this story is to talk to many people and let them know what services you offer. Find out if they offer services you could use. Then you never know, you might find yourself in a great position to barter.

Not offering services to your customers all year long.

I was reading a post on outdoor holiday decorations and it amazes me more lawn care business owners aren't doing this. In the post we were talking about the experience one lawn care business owner had with outdoor holiday lighting. His first year wasn't a big deal. He just wanted to get his feet wet with it and marketed it only to his current customer base by calling them up and using flyers.

After a few years, he is now seeing a 20% growth each year in his holiday decoration business.

An interesting way to market this service is to take photos of a commercial or residential building and use some graphic software to show how the building would look after you decorated it. We read on the forum, time and time again how you need to present your potential customers with imagery to help sell your concept. When you do this you need to go big with the design and the bid price. You can always scale down later if they request it. Leave it up to the customer to decide if what you presented is too over budget otherwise you may never know what the cost ceiling was you could have reached with them.

Your main business will be mid October to mid January. Shoot for a 40% profit margin. Also try and go for the larger projects that start around $750 and up. When you first get started playing with this you may be looking to charge around $500, but each year you do it, try and raise the price with more creative designs.

If you are interested in offering such services. You can play around with a graphics program to get some great proposal images.

- Step 1. Take a photo of the house during the day.

- Step 2. Create a new layer in your graphic program and lower the brightness to make it look dark.

- Step 3. Use the eraser and remove the dark area where the lights will be placed.

- Step 4. Add an airbrush light color, such as yellow, blue green, or red highlight.

- Step 5. Then use a smaller airbrush to add a white highlight.

- Step 6. Add some wreaths. You can get pictures of wreaths from anywhere on the web.

- Step 7. Add some lighted deers for the front yard and you are all set to submit a proposal.

After all this you will have a final image to present to the home owner or the commercial property manager to get final approval.

Not knowing the average direct mail response rate.

Most lawn care business owner's experiment with direct mail for their lawn care marketing and often wonder what kind of response rate they should be seeing.

Justin sent out mailings for his lawn care business and asked this very question on the Gopher Lawn Care Business Forum.

Justin's flyers were for a stump removal promotion he was offering. He asked "I've sent 475 color flyers on Wednesday and I only received 1 estimate so far.

I've seen most of my flyers in the garbage can at the post office, so does this mean people are tired of flyers?"

Bob responded by saying "No, that is actually a reasonable response from 475 flyers.

A good industry standard for direct mail is 1-2% response rate. But I'll tell you it's been a long time since I've seen a 1% response from my mailings. So at 1% you should have gotten about 4.75 calls. That might seem a little low…

However… You are marketing a service that is VERY unique. I don't know how it is in your area, but there just are not that many stumps that need to be ground down. For example if you did a flyer for "grass cutting" lets say, you know that just about everyone who sees your flyer, (or if you distribute them you can make sure) has a lawn. You don't know if everyone who saw your flyer has a stump that needs ground down. So you have shrunk your market. The same would be as if you marketed dog fence installation. If you mailed to every home in a neighborhood, you have no idea who has a dog or not. Even though your flyer has other services on it, the only thing that customer see is the "stump grinding."

Since customers only look at these thing for a split second, they are not seeing anything else but the main selling point. If they are interested in that, they might look at your other services, but not unless they want the main service your offering on the flyer. Does that make sense?

So I say if you got one response from 475 postcards, that is a good response rate. I think many people don't realize how many flyers, postcards, door hangers, or whatever... it really takes to really get a large number of sales.

Don't get frustrated, keep putting them out!!!"

Not striping lawns when you can.

James posted a great question on the Gopher Lawn Care Business Forum that you can join in on here. He asked "is striping lawns a normal service?"

Tom: "I think it depends on where you are. In the south, grasses such as bermuda and zoysia do not stripe well at all because of their growth habits "runner grasses". Although you can "burn" stripes in runner grasses. You just cut the exact same pattern every time you cut the lawn and eventually it shows up. but its not good for the grass to do this. In the south fescue will stripe well but that's about it. If you are in an area where you can grow rye grass fescue Kentucky blue etc "clump grasses", you can make striping look nice.

It is also one the most efficient way in terms of time to mow. You make a pass turn 180* and make a pass next to it. But you have to make sure you keep the mower straight. No one wants banana shaped stripes.

In my opinion I think it comes down to the type of grass you are cutting and if the owner wants it.

When you see stripes in grass you are seeing where the mower past. If the mower was going away from you it shows up as a light stripe. if the mower was coming towards you it makes a dark stripe."

Ken: "Striping a lawn is a great touch especially for customers in higher priced neighborhoods when you can charge for the extra effort needed to make stripes look professional.

Specific grasses and well irrigated lawns make for better stripes."

So always remember to make the lawns you service look the best they can. Your customer's lawn ultimately is a billboard to promote your lawn care service abilities.

I hope all these stories and insights have helped broaden and expand your business mind. Take all you have read here and go out and apply it. When you learn something new or interesting, please get on the Gopher Forum and share it with all of us. We'd love to hear what you have to say.

Until the next time, always remember to Dream it, Build it, Gopher it!